Thomas Cook

TRAVELLERS

SARDINIA

By
LIN

Written by Lindsay Bennett, updated by Marc di Duca
Original photography by Pete Bennett, updated photography by Marc di Duca

Published by Thomas Cook Publishing
A division of Thomas Cook Tour Operations Limited.
Company registration no. 1450464 England
The Thomas Cook Business Park, 9 Coningsby Road,
Peterborough PE3 8SB, United Kingdom
E-mail: books@thomascook.com, Tel: + 44 (0) 1733 416477
www.thomascookpublishing.com

Produced by Cambridge Publishing Management Limited
Burr Elm Court, Main Street, Caldecote CB23 7NU

ISBN: 978-1-84157-926-9

Series Editor: Linda Bass
Production/DTP: Steven Collins

Printed and bound in Italy by Printer Trento

Cover photography: Front L–R: © Ripani Massimo/SIME-4 Corners Images;
© Leplat Veronique/SIME-4 Corners Images; © Ripani Massimo/SIME-4
Corners Images; Back L–R: © Leplat Veronique/SIME-4 Corners Images;
© Fantuz Olimpio/SIME-4 Corners Images.

Although every care has been taken in compiling this publication, and the

Thomas Cook Tour
rors or omissions,
ebook, or for the
. Descriptions and
es when writing and
)perations Limited.

fied as having
d or fibre

Trento S.r.l.,
d paper in
elling standards.

FSC

Mixed Sources
Product group from well-managed
forests and recycled wood or fibre
Cert no. CQ-COC-000012
www.fsc.org
© 1996 Forest Stewardship Council

Contents

KEY TO MAPS

✈	Airport
★	Start of walk/tour
1250m ▲	Mountain
i	Information
✝	Church
☀	Viewpoint
SS197	Road number

Introduction

It is said that the Mediterranean is spoiled for travellers; that mass tourism and the modern machinations of the European Union have homogenised its cultures and that the package business has left nowhere new to discover. But this is wrong – there is still Sardinia, an Italian island of untold delights and amazing natural beauty.

The island's magnificent coastline is its most stunning asset. From cosy rocky inlets to vast strands, the golden beaches are caressed by azure waters that make an excellent playground for bronzers and for the yachtsmen whose white-masted vessels anchored offshore only add to the picture-perfect vista.

The beaches protect hectares of coastal lagoons offering an inviting home to flamingoes and other visiting birds. This is where the sand stops and the granite and limestone begin, their surface eroded into surreal shapes and cut by numerous caverns.

Nature's raw material has been in good hands for centuries, sculpted by man since before the Bronze Age. History has cast a long and languorous shadow here and you can spend more than a day or two clambering around dusty historical sites. Sardinia's Nuraghic peoples have left us a remarkable legacy: unique architecture and a wealth of beautiful and intricate

objects that rewrite the script on ancient life.

However, since 500 BC Sardinians have seen power-brokers from the rest of Europe come and go while they have tended their flocks and cast their nets. While sheep were kings on land, tuna ruled the seas, and the annual *mattanza*, the bloody tuna harvest where men overcome these 100kg (220lb) fish with their bare hands, epitomises the islanders' struggle with and respect for nature's bounty.

Ties with the island's traditions are still strong even in the face of 21st-century modernity, and tourism seems to flow with this tradition rather than crowding it out. Many of Sardinia's festivals have been passed down through the centuries, yet today they are undertaken with great reverence by Vespa-riding youths who, on all other days of the year, sport designer sunglasses and the latest 'threads'. Perhaps the most famed region of Sardinia is the exclusive Costa Smeralda with its smattering of celebrities and a surfeit of blue-blooded Europeans. But while the marina at Porto Cervo, its main resort, might be a byword for expense, the rest of the island can be tackled without a constant eye on one's bank balance.

Tremendously skilled with their hands, Sardinians produce a vast range of handicrafts. These everyday items eschew mass production in favour of small-scale artisan quality at prices that don't make you squirm. They also have a local cuisine that is markedly different from the mainland, with succulent suckling pig or roast lamb with just a hint of rosemary. You don't have to look off island for wine either; domestic reds, whites and rosés from dry to sweet and light to robust are delicious; and the cold pressed extra virgin olive oil, the basis of every dish, is exquisite.

The colourful hillside houses of Posada

Every August Sardinians see an invasion from the east as their Italian compatriots take over, intent on having fun and soaking up the sun. But aside from this month of mayhem you will find space and a place to relax, plus a refreshingly unpretentious and interesting destination that will stay in your memory long after you return home.

Introduction

Coastal Sardinia is like an artist's palette of cooling colours

The land

'Sardinian land, red, bitter, virile, woven into a carpet of stars, since time immemorial, blossoming unblemished every spring, a primordial cradle where I felt its calm rocking the sea.'

ERNST JÜNGER
Terra Sarda

Basics of geography

With a total area of just over 24,000sq km (9,265sq miles) Sardinia is a lot of land for its population of one and a half million and it is a wonderfully varied landscape to enjoy. The long coastline ranges from sweeping stretches of beach and coastal lagoons to rocky peninsulas and high cliffscapes. Though none of its peaks break 2,000m (6,560ft), the ridges and summits at the heart of the Gennargentu, the only large area of high ground, give the impression of altitude. In the north, around Porto Torres, and the central west around Oristano are flat plains that are the breadbasket of the island. There are several rivers – called by the Spanish name *rio* in the north – but only one, the Temo, is navigable to any length.

Flora

The island displays a large range of species because of the varied environments created by the topography and climate, though, as you would expect, there is a predominance of Mediterranean plants, with a smattering of North African types. Only a small amount of ancient forest remains, but there are vast tracts of cork oak and various types of olive that have been cultivated – perhaps as far back as Roman times – and then gone wild. Pine forest backs some tracts of sand and you will even find an ancient petrified forest on the shores of Lake Omodeo.

The *garriga* – low-growing scrub that blankets non-forested and non-cultivated areas – is a mixture of wild herbs, tough grasses, Balearic box, juniper, broom and the dwarf palm, on the western coast. This palm is an ancient species found in the Tertiary period that has been appropriated by the Sardinians to make basketware. Another, in a similar vein, is the lentisk. Grasses are not the only profitable wild plants here; the fruits of the myrtle and the arbutus (of the strawberry family) are eaten fresh or distilled into a liqueur. There is an abundance of nuts too – almond, hazel and walnut – and the succulent prickly pear, though not native, is now widespread.

The countryside is a carpet of wild flowers in the spring and these include species of iris and miniature orchid. The show starts pretty early in the spring and is over by mid-May, when the sun gets too hot for the flowers to thrive. There is another mini-blanket of flowers in October, when the first showers of autumn awaken the seeds.

Sardinia regions

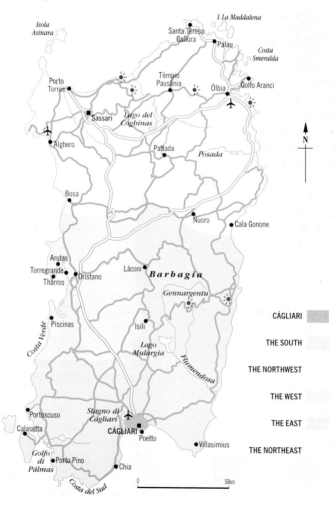

The land

Date palm

Fauna

The landmass of Sardinia is large enough to have sustained populations of many wild creatures, but there is also a long tradition of hunting, which gained momentum as the human population grew. This sport has unfortunately reduced the numbers of many creatures to danger levels. The mouflon is the most impressive of these animals. The tough wild 'sheep' with its majestic horns is found also in Corsica and in the high Alps. The horn has traditionally been used to fabricate the handles on Sardinian knives.

Sardinian deer (*Cervo sardo*) are smaller than their mainland cousins and, although once widespread, now inhabit specially protected stretches of woodland. Experts say there are only a few hundred of the deer left. The same is true of the Sardinian wild boar (*Cinghiale sardo*), which is again a diminutive form. Numbers dropped to such low levels that larger mainland boar have been introduced, but the interbreeding of the two species will obviously change the bloodline. However, numbers are less of a concern than in the case of the deer.

Nor are humans the only hunters on the island. Though Sardinia has no large carnivores, it has voracious martens and red-footed weasels, and the dark-bellied fox is a wily opportunist. Hunters also roam the skies, with several large species of birds of prey thriving here.

On any stroll around an ancient site or medieval castle, you will be accompanied by the scurry of departing lizards. Sardinia has a wide range, including some only found on the island. This includes the gongilo lizard and *Discoplossus pictus*, a cross between a frog and a toad. Scientists have shown that the *Geotritone sardo* was walking these same lands back in the Miocene era. Less numerous and almost never seen is the Sardinian tortoise.

The people

Sardinian by birth and Italian simply by accident of geography, most natives have a deep and abiding love

EQUINE STOCKS

The wild Sardinian horse is a unique sub-species and still roams free around the south central Giara region of the island. This is a miniature breed and not any bigger than the size of a pony.

for their island. Perhaps it is the eons of subjugation, exploitation and over-taxation that have created the invisible bond. Or perhaps the sheer distance from any mainland European territory has promoted an independent spirit that continues to this day. Family and community ties are close knit, but this is beginning to break down with the greater mobility of people in recent times. Currently, the island is experiencing a net loss of population as young people head to the mainland in search of greater economic opportunities.

Sardinians are generally more reserved than their mainland compatriots and a little less hot-blooded. They have an easier-going and more relaxed temperament, and one of the most obvious signs of this is in their driving style. There is far less horn honking and quick acceleration here, and much more patience and consideration at junctions or in car parks than, say, in Milan or Turin.

The harbour at Alghero

Sardinian beaches

It may sound like an overstatement, but Sardinia can truly claim to have the best beaches in the Mediterranean and its coastline can stand up against anything the Caribbean has to offer. There is a beach for everyone here. Sand ranges from the consistency of powder to small marble balls, and in colour from pale pink, through golden yellow to almost white.

Some of the best beaches offer excellent facilities so you can get lunch or drinks, hire windsurfing boards or kayaks and enjoy banana-boat rides, while others simply offer what nature blessed them with. You can have as much company as you want or find a stretch of sand with no one else in sight. As a general rule of thumb, the further a beach is from the towns the quieter it will be and the fewer facilities will be provided. Here are some of the best:

Arutas (north of Tharros)
The most unusual sand, Arutas is made up of hectares of marble rocks ground round and smooth by the action of the waves, some the size of sugar crystals, others as big as peppercorns. The stone shines a translucent white in the sunshine and the beach stretches for several kilometres.

Cala Gonone
Backed by 900m (2,950ft) peaks, Cala Gonone was only reachable by boat until the latter part of the 20th century. Today the road has brought new development to the bay but the setting is impressive, and it is a jumping-off point to other remote coves along the eastern coast.

Chia (south of Pula)
A long sandy stretch, this beach is excellent for beach walks. The northern sector is one of the most popular for surfers and windsurfers: a

Windsurfing at Chia beach

One of the island's many sheltered coves

great spectator sport. The further west you walk, the quieter it becomes.

A couple of bars at the beach entrance provide refreshments. And if you are looking for more than just a snack, there are resort hotels with fine dining, including good wine.

Piscinas (on the Costa Verde)

Piscinas village anchors a long sandy stretch on one of the least visited shores on the island.

Poetto

The longest and widest beach on the island, Poetto is also one of the closest to Cágliari so you will never have it to yourself, but you do not come here for solitude. This is a beach to see and be seen on, especially for the young and trendy. A line of fashionable bars backs the sand, and socialites meet here at weekends to enjoy a long seafood lunch.

Porto Pino
(on the southwest coast)

This is part of a fine curved, gently shelving bay. Just next door is a narrow inlet full of gently bobbing fishing boats. Cross the wooden bridge to reach Porto Pino village with its cafés and restaurants.

Torregrande (north of Oristano)

In the sheltered Golfo di Oristano, with gently shelving sand and tiny waves, Torregrande is great for children. You can walk for several kilometres along the shoreline, which is backed by pine forests and lagoons.

Villasimius (on the southeast tip of Sardinia)

A long sandy spit backed by a saltwater lagoon, Villasimius is another beach where you can choose to stay close to the cafés and bars or walk south to more private stretches.

History

Before 10,000 BC Some finds from man's earliest ancestors have been found at Perfugas in Sassari province, dating from the Upper Palaeolithic period. Lower Palaeolithic tools have been found at Oliena in Nuoro province.

c. **3500– 2700 BC** The Ozieri culture flourishes during the Neolithic age. They constructed over 300 'Dómus de Janus' or 'house of the fairies' tomb complexes where they laid their dead. The Ozieri evolved a highly developed culture over several generations.

c. **2700 BC** Transition period as other tribes arrive in Ozieri territory.

c. **1600 BC** The Nuraghic peoples make Sardinia their home. They are most remembered for their conical towers or *nuraghi*, of which there are over 7,000 on the island. Over time the Nuraghi begin to trade with other cultures, including the Phoenicians and the Egyptians.

c. **1000 BC** The Phoenicians arrive and settle on the island, founding cities at Bithia, Karalis, Nora Sulcis and Tharros, trading with the late Nuraghic peoples. The name 'Shrdn' is coined by these settlers, which eventually evolves into the name Sardegna or Sardinia.

900–500 BC Late Nuraghic civilisation is highly advanced, as witnessed by the *bronzetti*, beautifully detailed small bronze statues depicting people and objects, such as ships and animals, that have been found in large numbers at archaeological sites around the island.

509 BC The Phoenicians from Carthage take control of the island, introducing their religious customs and pushing the Nuraghic peoples into the hinterland; starting the pastoral tradition of the countryfolk that lasts to this day.

227 BC Rome vanquishes Carthage and takes over the Phoenician cities and founds the port at Porto Torres. Unrest among Sardinians continues until the early years of the 1st century AD.

27 BC Sardinia becomes a senatorial province of Rome.

AD 212 Sardinians granted Roman citizenship.

303 St Efisio and other important early Christians are martyred by Emperor Diocletian. Despite the eventual spread of Christianity, pagan rituals do not die out.

455 After the fall of the Roman Empire, the Sardinian coast is overrun by the Vandals.

534 Sardinia is taken by the Eastern Christian Byzantines (based in Constantinople, now Istanbul), but their grip on territories so far away from home is not firm. Raids by Moors and Arabs are common in the 8th and 9th centuries and Byzantium finally retreats from the island.

9th century Sardinia begins an era of self-determination, when the island is divided into four districts called 'Giudicati' (Arborea, Cágliari, Gallura and Torres), ruled by *giudici* or judges. Both the Sardinian language and an island code of law are established.

***c.* 12th century** The island comes to the attention of rising feudal power bases both east and west. In 1157 a *giudice* from Arborea marries into the Aragonese fiefdom.

1187 Pisa and Genoa on the northern Italian mainland take control of three of the Giudicati.

1238 Enzo, son of Frederick II, is given the title King of Sardinia, and marries the daughter of the *giudice* of Cágliari province.

1294 Pope Boniface offers two regions of Sardinia and the whole of Corsica to James II of Aragon.

1297 The city of Sassari places itself under Genoese protection.

1323	Alphonse of Aragon begins a campaign to take the whole island. Though he concludes a peace deal with Pisa in 1326, the islanders fight on against the 'invaders'.
1353	The Aragonese consolidate power in the northwest by founding Alghero.
1380s	Eleonora of Arborea leads a popular revolt against the Aragonese until she dies of the plague in 1402.
1409	The Battle of Sanluri leads to the surrender of the Arborea Giudicati.
1400s	The marriage of Ferdinand and Isabella in 1469 cements the ties between the house of Aragon and the Spanish house of Castille. This family line develops into the greatest bloodline in Europe, the Habsburgs.
The early 1500s	Sardinia is plagued by pirate raids.
1541	Habsburg Emperor Charles V visits the island.
1706	The King of Spain dies without an heir, plunging Europe into war.
1714	After the War of the Spanish Succession, the Treaty of Utrecht cedes Sardinia to the Austrian crown.
1717	The Spanish retake the island.
1720	The island passes to Savoy in the Piedmontese region of Italy, ushering in one of the most difficult periods in the island's modern history, with high taxation and poverty.
1794	Popular rebellion against rule by Savoy.
1799	Napoleon invades Savoy and the ruling family retreats, to Sardinia. French forces are pushed back after landing on the Sardinian coast.
1847	The population requests union with Piedmont.
1855	Giuseppe Garibaldi buys one of the Maddalena islands.

1861   The Kingdom of Italy is created, uniting many of the old feudal city-states and regions in one state. Sardinia fights against this and many die.

1868   Rural uprising in Nuoro.

1889   The military is brought in to quash banditry.

1914–18   The Brigata Sassari is famed for its bravery and fighting prowess in defence of the Italian state during World War I.

1921   The Partido Sardo d'Azione begins a campaign for the island's independence.

1930s   Mussolini invests heavily in mining in the southwest of the island, creating jobs and income.

1940–45   Cágliari and Olbia are bombed during World War II.

1945   Italy becomes a republic.

1948   Sardinia becomes an autonomous region within the Italian state.

1960s   The first seeds of tourism on the islands.

1970s   The Costa Smeralda is developed.

1970s–1990s   A series of kidnappings and ransoms of wealthy and influential islanders.

1985   Sardinian Francesco Cossiga becomes president of Italy.

1990   Cágliari becomes one of the region's venues when Italy hosts football's World Cup.

2008   Following an agreement between the Italian and US governments, the US nuclear submarine base at Santo Stefano in the Maddalena Islands closes in February 2008.

The Palazzo Viceregio was first erected in the 15th century and today houses the Provincial Assembly

Ancient structures

Between the 16th century BC and the arrival of the Romans in the 3rd century BC, Sardinia was home to the unique and sophisticated peoples of the Nuraghic culture, named after the tall stone towers that are a constant feature of their settlements. There are over 7,000 *nuraghe* towers on the island and they are found nowhere else on earth, though the structures are related to others found in Corsica and the Balearic islands of Mallorca and Menorca.

The word *nuraghe* (plural *nuraghi*) comes from the Sardinian word 'nurra' meaning 'hollow building' or 'hollow pile'. *Nuraghi* can be tholos style: a conical tower with an interior chamber, which is the most common style; or corridor style: a series of corridors leading to a corbelled roof chamber.

Some towers stand sentinel, but others are surrounded by the remains of Nuraghic villages, masses of small round stone cottages that once sported thatch roofs.

Tombs

The Nuraghi used megalithic communal burial sites of two main types. The first was the Giant's Tomb.

All these have a slim rectangular main chamber, lined with stone, also called a 'dolmen cist', and a curved façade comprising huge flat-shaped stone slabs. The longest one on the island is over 23m (75ft) in length. These tombs would be covered with an earth mound.

The second were more complex carved caves – there are over 300 so far identified on the island. Tombs have been found with up to 200 skeletons, though scientists are not yet sure whether bodies were placed here to rot or whether the skeletons were placed inside once the flesh had decayed. Protector stones or memorial stones were placed close to the entrance.

Bronzetti

These small bronze sculptures are, along with the towers, the most

Necropoli di Li Mur

Nuraghe d'Albucciu in Arzachena

striking gift that the Nuraghi left the Sardinians. *Bronzetti* were inspired by all aspects of Nuraghic life during their creative heyday between the 9th and the 3rd centuries BC. They smelted bronzes of themselves, their boats, their animals, their weapons and even their towers in sizes that range from just over 2cm (¾in) to just under 40cm (15¾in). Some were used as objects of veneration and as objects of pleasure and they have been found in homes, caves and tombs. The major collection is on display in the National Archaeological Museum in Cágliari (*see p44*).

Nuraghe Su Nuraxi

The most complete Nuraghic site, Nuraghe Su Nuraxi (*see p85*), in the foothills of the Gennargentu, has been added to the list of UNESCO World Heritage Sites because the selection committee decided that this *nuraghe* represents an exceptional use of the materials and techniques that were available to a prehistoric island community.

Important vocabulary

Allée couverte – a simple long rectangular hole lined and topped with stone, into which a body or skeleton was interred.

Dolmen – a tomb topped by a single huge slab of stone.

Dómus de Janus – small artificial caves used as tombs. There are over 300 on the island.

Menhir – a tall upright stone erected as a marker.

Necropolis – an area of land specially given over to the dead.

Well temples – a tholos is built over a freshwater well or source where water cult followers worshipped.

Politics

The Italian political arena has seen more scandals than a soap opera and more twists and turns than a John Le Carré novel. It is dominated by powerful and charismatic businessmen pitting their wits against a plethora of lawyers or academics turned social crusaders, on top of which is the ever-present influence of the Catholic Church.

Since 1946 Italy's multi-party and proportional representation system has resulted in decades of short-lived and ineffectual governments, fractured by factional in-fighting and made worse by corruption scandals (*see pp20–21*) that have shocked the population and brought public confidence in politicians to an all-time low.

Palazzo Viceregio, Cágliari

In the 1990s things came to a head and vox populi voted in sweeping changes to the electoral system to improve consensus and longevity. Proportional representation was to a great extent replaced by a 'first past the post' system and parties must now take four per cent of the national vote to enter parliament.

The party system also changed irrevocably in the mid-90s, with the demise of the powerful Christian Democratic Party and the arrival of Forza Italia led by Silvio Berlusconi.

A touch of history

The Italian State was ratified in 1861 under King Vittorio Emanuele II. A parliamentary democracy until the early 1920s and the coming of Mussolini, Italy was ruled by dictatorship until the fall of the Fascist regime and the end of World War II, when a democratic republic was established by popular referendum. The current constitution was ratified in 1948.

Olbia Town Hall

The structure

The legislative structure is a two-tier parliament, a Chamber of Deputies with 630 members and a Senate with 315 members. Both houses are elected for a maximum of five years, but the Senate has some members – political luminaries – who are appointed for life. Seventy-five per cent of the seats are filled by a 'first past the post' method, while the remaining twenty-five per cent are filled by proportional representation.

Parliament elects the president, the figurehead of the country. The president then nominates the prime minister, who in turn chooses individuals for ministerial portfolios within the Council of Ministers, the inner cabinet.

Silvio Berlusconi

The head of a huge business empire, encompassing food, construction, TV, newspapers and even football, it is hard to find an element of Italian life that

Berlusconi does not have a finger in. Born in 1936 in Milan, he graduated in law but started in business as a property developer, with a loan from a bank where his father worked. He moved into cable television a decade later and then into newspapers. In 1993, in response to the public outcry against the Milan corruption scandal, he formed Forza Italia, 'Go Italy', named, it is said, after a chant used on the terraces of his football club AC Milan. He has served two terms as prime minister and, despite losing the 2006 election to Romano Prodi, Berlusconi remains one of Italy's most powerful figures.

Corruption

Since the founding of the republic, Italy has been drowning in a sea of corruption. A look at the scene since 1990 reveals several shocking debacles.

In 1992, the discovery of a small backhander of less than £5,000 to a local official uncovered a web of corruption in Milan. Charges were brought against five former prime ministers and thousands of city officials.

In 1994, Silvio Berlusconi was forced to resign from government after investigations into his multi-billion dollar business dealings. His political ally businessman and former prime minister, Bettino Craxi, fled Italy for Tunisia, rather than face questioning. He died in exile in 2000.

In February 2000, four members of the Italian aid mission in Kosovo were charged with appropriating millions of dollars worth of aid meant for refugees, with the help of the Albanian mafia.

In 2001 Berlusconi escaped prosecution on charges stemming from investigations of corruption in the early 1990s because the Statute of Limitations had run out.

The UN Human Rights Commission started 2002 by announcing an investigation into the independence of the Italian judiciary.

May 2002 saw parliament approve a bill allowing Berlusconi to remain in 'hands-on control' of his media empire, including several TV companies and national newspapers, while undertaking the role of prime minister.

Berlusconi finally went on trial in May 2003 for allegations relating to business dealings in the 1980s, but

Commemorative plaque

Symbol of the Italian State

from many private homes and business establishments, but no one is really sure how the *quattro mori* – the heads of four Moors with flowing hair and a bandana in four squares separated by a red cross – should have come to represent the island. However the *mori* also feature in the flag of Corsica, Sardinia's close neighbour to the north, and this may have started with their long common history of subjugation.

parliament passed a new law in June 2003 approving immunity from prosecution for prime ministers and other leading politicians while they are still in position. However, in January 2004, the Italian Constitutional Court declared this law invalid.

In 2005, in a new trial, Berlusconi was acquitted of charges of bribery, and all other charges were dropped.

Sardinia

Under the 1948 constitution, Sardinia is one of five regions with a special autonomy within the modern state. The elected assembly has many powers over the day-to-day running of the island but is still ultimately responsible to central government in Rome. The council sits at the renovated Palazzo Viceregio in the Castello quarter in Cágliari.

The *quattro mori*

This curious symbol was approved as the national flag of the island in 1999. It flies from all public buildings and

Calls for independence

Since the fall of the Giudicati in medieval times, Sardinia has lived under the yoke of 'foreign power' and it was dragged into the greater Italian state by default. Even after the founding of the republic and the awarding of special autonomous status under the Italian constitution, there is still a feeling of being ignored by the powers in Rome.

Some would like to see Sardinia declare itself independent, as slogans in public places will prove. You will see them plastered across telegraph poles and the walls of abandoned buildings, but the movement is by no means as militant or vocal as, say, that of the Basques in Spain. Much grumbling tends to go on in general conversation at bars and cafés over an espresso or two, but with the money from tourism taking the edge off poverty on the island, the will for direct action and political revolution appears to have been dented, maybe for now or maybe for good.

Culture

Culture is a multi-faceted diamond on Sardinia. Washed over by the waves of artistic and cultural movements that have swept through Europe, it has safeguarded a rich core of tradition in festivals, music, dance and literature, keeping its own unique heartbeat alive.

Festivals

The festivals and religious *sagres* (processions) represent a continuity through the ages that has been lost in most parts of Europe. In many instances the timeline leads back beyond Christianity into the pagan past

Relief sculpture in Fertilia

and the Nuraghic peoples themselves with their nature deities and the celebration of the passing seasons.

Carnival is taken very seriously, especially in the interior, where farming traditions continue into the modern era. Oristano is host to one of the most famous and ancient festivals in Italy, La Sartiglia, which includes horse-riding feats and elaborate costumed parades and rituals (*see p80*).

In Mamoiada, the *Mamuthones* (costumed men) wander through the town with their black masks and shaggy sheepskins, carrying the *campanacci* (a group of cow bells that weigh over 30kg/66lbs) the clanging of the bells echoing through the streets. They are chased by *issohadores*, with their white masks and red uniform.

In a village close by, the *Mamuthones* are called *Mamuztones*, and, instead of masks, their faces are painted black and they wear tall cork hats. They dance around s'Urtzu, a half man, half goat character, who is then (traditionally a shepherd's instrument), the *tumbarino* drum and the *serraggia* (a cane pipe, pig's bladder and string that is played with a lentisk grass bow).

In modern times the dances are more usually accompanied by the melodeon, which was invented in Austria in the 1820s and brought to Italy in the 1860s.

Literature

Sardinian fiction has benefited from a real glut of talent over the last 120 years or so. Storylines always seem to touch on the themes of class and money, social justice, family ties and the gritty reality of farming and shepherding, often from the point of view of a narrator: the central character. Nuoro seems to have been particularly fertile ground for the literary imagination.

Bronze statue of writer Sebastiano Satta in Nuoro

Grazia Deledda (1871–1936)

Born into a well-to-do landowning family that was at the centre of a vast social circle, Deledda spent her youth surrounded by the people and activities that filled her later novels.

She had her first short story published while still of school age, and her first novel, *Flower of Sardinia*, appeared in 1892. *Elias Portolu* (1903) was the work that established her intenational reputation. She was awarded the Nobel Prize for Literature in 1926.

Sebastiano Satta (1867–1914)

Satta studied as a lawyer but was also an avid poet and had three collections

sacrificed. In Orotelli the blackened face belongs to Sos Thurpos, who imitates an animal in a yoke.

The essence of all these rituals is the traditional confrontation between good and evil, and villagers hope to scare away the evil spirits that lurk in the dark shadows of winter.

Music

The lamenting lilt of the Sardinian reed pipe or *launeddas* fills the air at festivals and celebrations. The instrument consists of three grass pipes of different lengths, each of which gives off different tones. Other instruments include the *su popiolu* or cane pipe

Mural depicting *Mamuthones*

published before his death, and a further posthumous collection. His poetry speaks of social injustice and the fate of victims such as the women left behind. Unfortunately, Satta suffered from his own economic and family problems and also from poor health. He was paralysed for the last six years of his life.

Antioco Casula (1878–1957)

Regarded as the greatest lyrical poet to write in the Sardinian language, Casula was close to Sebastiano Satta and started his working life as a police officer. His own life was touched by tragedy when one child and his wife died young. He represented Sardinia at the first National Congress of the Italian dialects in 1925.

Gavino Ledda (1938–)

Perhaps the best-known Sardinian writer currently still living is Gavino Ledda, whose book *Padre, Padrone* (1979) is based on his own early life as an illiterate shepherd.

Art

For most of its artistic treasures, Sardinia followed the lead of its Spanish or Italian political masters, but some native names shine through, and, as with the written word, the 20th century brought some island talent to the attention of the world.

Pietro Cavaro (?–1538)

The most famous of the Stampace School of artists, Cavaro was born in Barcelona and worked in Naples before arriving in Cágliari. His work is a melding of the Catalan style with Renaissance sentiments, seen best in *The Mercy of Tangari*. His powerful works can be seen at the Pinacoteca Nazionale in Cágliari and the Antiquarium Arborense in Oristano, or the *Retablo della Crocifissione* in the dome of the cathedral in Cágliari.

Mario Delitala (1887–1990)

Born in Orani, Delitala qualified as an accountant and moved to Milan in 1907 to learn lithography but was an amateur artist and began exhibiting his work. In 1912 he returned to Cágliari, where his artistic life took over from his trained profession. He studied in Venice but returned to Sardinia and worked on pieces for the dome of the church in Lanusei and for the Alghero cathedral. After World War II, Delitala became director of the art institute in Palermo but continued to decorate churches, including the parish church at Orani. He retired to Sassari in 1961 but did not stop painting until his death in 1990, at the age of 103.

Constantino Nìvola (1911–88)

Born in the Barbagia to a poor rural family, Nìvola started his working life as a stonemason but moved to Milan and studied at the State Institute for Artistic Industry in Monza, where he put on his first sculpture exhibition.

He then moved on to Paris, where he met his wife, American Ruth Guggenheim. In 1936 he moved back to Italy but left the country after racial laws were introduced: his wife was Jewish. The couple travelled to the USA, where Nìvola worked on pieces for major corporations and became great friends with Le Corbusier.

The essence of his work was that he moved with ease between sculpture and architecture.

In 1954 he became a professor and director of the Design Workshop at Harvard, and in 1972 he was admitted as the first non-American member of the American Academy of Arts and Letters.

POP ART?

At Orgosolo, street murals became one way to protest against the social problems and inequalities inherent in Sardinian society and they attracted a lot of publicity in the 1970s. Today, however, they are more often a way for young artists to get on the first rung of the career ladder.

Sculpture park in Teulada

Architectural styles

The history of colonial stewardship of Sardinia brought many architectural styles to the island. If you are not sure what is Romanesque or Renaissance, here is a quick guide to post-ancient Roman architectural styles.

Early Christian/Byzantine

Named after Byzantium (or Constantinople), the capital of the Christian world in the late first millennium, this religious style used a rectangular ground plan with a simple open structure and entrance from the west. Chiesa di San Saturno in Cágliari (*see p41*) and San Giovanni di Sinis near Oristano (*see p83*) still have the core structure of this style.

Romanesque bell tower

Romanesque

This 11th- and 12th-century style harks back to ancient Rome; in fact, many shaped stones were recycled from Roman sites in the initial phases. Arches had rounded tops and were relatively small and narrow, with columns carved as a decorative feature.

Northern Sardinia is brimful with Romanesque masterpieces; most were built by the Pisans in their distinctive contrasting layers of black and white stone. Chiesa di San Pietro di Sorres (*see p109*) and Chiesa SS Trinita Saccargia (*see p98*) are just two examples of Pisan Romanesque style.

Gothic

The Gothic style was a development of the Romanesque and its main feature is the pointed arch, which became extremely fine as the style developed. In churches and cathedrals, the western façade was the most impressive exterior feature, and these became more and more ornate over time. Many of Sardinia's early churches were upgraded during the Gothic era, but Chiesa di Sant'Eulalia in Cágliari (*see p42*) is of unadulterated Catalan-Gothic design.

Copper panel in a church

Renaissance

The Renaissance or 'rebirth' revolutionised the arts in the 14th–16th centuries. The architectural style again harked back to the Roman classics, including the four styles of columns and the arch. Sardinia has relatively few mainstream Renaissance buildings, though the Chiesa di Sant'Agostino in Cágliari (see p39) is the prime example.

Baroque

The baroque style was fashionable from the late 16th to the mid-18th century and is characterised by ornate decoration with the aid of columns, domes, pilasters and entablature. Sardinia has many older churches that were refurbished in baroque style, such as the Duomo in Cágliari (see pp38–9). Other churches that were built during the era are the Chiesa di Sant'Anna and Chiesa di San Michele in Cágliari (see p40).

Rococo

Rococo describes the most ornate phase of baroque, when flamboyant decoration played on every surface, particularly cornices and pediments. The Chiesa del Carmine in Bosa (see p95) is a fine example.

Neoclassical

A backlash against baroque in the late 18th century brought the purer lines, now called the neoclassical style. The main characteristics are clean and uncluttered lines, based on the mathematical formulae used by the ancient Greeks. This era coincided with an expansion of Italian confidence and the building of vast governmental palaces, such as the Municipio in Sassari (see pp104–6).

Modernism

During the 1930s the Mussolini regime saw architecture as one way to promote the modernisation of the country and ploughed vast amounts of money into official buildings; the functionalism of towns like Arborea (see p74) and Fertilia (see p103) are good examples.

Festivals and events

Tradition plays an important part in Sardinian life, especially out in the countryside, where even today the days flow with the seasons and the main religious festivals. The year is filled with community activities, many with a long pedigree. The major festivals are listed here, but the tourist office is bound to have information about others happening during your visit.

January
Festival of Sant Abate
Festival with pagan roots. Bonfires are lit in many villages in Nuoro, particularly in Orosei, Mamoiada and Torpè, and there is a blessing with the fire. *16 January.*

The black-masked *Mamuthones* roam the streets at Mamoiada (Nuoro province). *17 January.*

February and March
Elaborate Carnival rituals are held in Oristano and in towns all across the Gennargentu. These feature traditional masks and dances dating back to pagan times (*see pp22–3 and p80*). The events at Mamoiada are repeated to usher in a new year.

April
Sardinia Day
Celebration of the Sardinian Vespers, a popular uprising in 1794 that brought about banishment of the Piedmontese. *28 April.*

May
Festival of Sant'Efisio
A spectacular procession with *traccas* (decorated ox-carts), begun in 1656. Procession from Cágliari to Nora (Cágliari province). *1–4 May.*

June
San Giovanni Battista
Several different festivals. Sheep festivals in Bauladu or Milis in Oristano province. Horses are ridden bareback through the streets at Paulitano or Bonarcado, also in Oristano province. *24 June.*

July
S'Ardia
A gruelling horse race between dozens of horses and riders through the streets of Sedilo (Oristano province) on the festival of St Constantino. *6–7 July.*

August
Medieval Parade
Parade with traditional costumes dating from the period of Conte Ugolino della

Gherardesca's rule. Iglesias (Cágliari province). *13 August.*

Festa dell'Assunta e Palio di Santa Maria

14 August sees 14 local bachelors attempting to catch a heifer. On the 15th the town holds the Palio di Santa Maria horse race through the town. Guasila (Cágliari province). *14–15 August.*

I Canelieri

In a 700-year-old celebration, three huge candelabra are carried through the town. Nulvi (Sassari province). *14 August.*

On the same day the representatives of the traditional craft guilds race through the town carrying candles. In Sassari there is a festival in the city.

Feast of the Assumption

Huge island-wide celebrations but especially at Orgoloso (Nuoro province), with a costumed parade and horse races. *15 August.*

Sant'Ignazio da Láconi

A religious procession with costumed folkloric activities. *Last weekend of the month.*

Festa del Redentore

One of the best festivals of the year featuring a range of traditional costumes, *traccas* (decorated ox-carts), folk music and a song contest. *Last Sunday of the month.*

September

Festival of San Salvatore (*see p83*)

Hundreds of young men run barefoot in a re-enactment of the fight against the Saracens. Followed by a religious procession. Cabras (Oristano province). *First Sunday of the month.*

Santa Greca

Festival with traditional food and music at Decimomannu (Cágliari province). *Last Sunday of the month.*

October

Chestnut Festival

Costumed parade and food festival featuring the chestnut at Aritzo (Nuoro province). *Last Sunday of the month.*

November

Arts and Crafts Festival

Handicrafts, traditional music and art exhibitions plus a Sardinian poetry competition and s'Istrumpa wrestling. Désulo (Nuoro province). *1–5 November.*

December

Signum Judicii

A traditional medieval chant of Aragonese origin in Alghero's cathedral. *24 December.*

Sa Pertusitta, Sa Zuada and Su Cabue

A traditional mass, followed by a festival blessing the local bread. Goceano (Sassari province). *30 December.*

Festivals and events

Impressions

'Siesta is prime time for Italian TV. It is prime time for sex, too. Maybe this accounts for the Mediterranean temperament versus the northern one: children conceived in the light and children conceived in the dark.'

FRANCES MAYES
Under the Tuscan Sun, 1998

Where is it?

The island of Sardinia, or Sardegna in Italian, sits in the heart of the western Mediterranean, a surprising distance from the western coast of mainland Italy. The northern tip appears to kiss the island of Corsica and from the capital, Cágliari, in the south you could almost throw a stick at Tunisia on the north coast of Africa.

When to go

Sardinia has something to offer no matter what the season. Though it is advertised as a sunbather's paradise – and that is certainly true – the cultural treasures await throughout the year and the activities for which the island is gaining a growing reputation are better enjoyed without the fierce heat of high summer.

Spring

As the hours of daylight get longer, native birds burst into song and migratory birds arrive on the journey north, spending a few weeks in the many lakes and marshes. Spring wheat blankets the fields, myriad flowers fill the hedgerows and flocks are released into the hills for another year at around the same time as the forest of umbrellas opens at pavement cafés all over the island and hotel shutters open for another year's trading. The temperature is perfect for all kinds of activities from trekking to mountain biking. The occasional storm can spoil the weather and evenings are still cool.

Summer

Once the wheat has been cut and the days get hotter, the ground turns dry and parched. Beach concessions get out their wares and by mid-July the race is on to obtain the last remaining vacant rooms around the island. Ferries and flights from the Italian mainland don't have any spare capacity and restaurants burst at the seams. Daytime temperatures rise to over 37°C (100°F) every day, so it is not wise to get too active, but it makes for a sizzling suntan. Evenings are long, languid and sticky; though maybe too uncomfortable for sleep without air conditioning.

Summer is also *festa* time, when the costumes worn in hundreds of processions throughout the island hark back to generations past.

Autumn

Perhaps late summer and early autumn are the best time to visit. The heat of August is tempered, but the days are still wonderfully warm and the ground seems to radiate the heat it stored through the longest summer days. When the first showers arrive, flowers and grasses spring anew, leaving the countryside verdant and colourful

again. Flamingoes and other migratory birds arrive once more for a brief sojourn.

Winter

When the last package tourists leave at the end of October, life takes on a different pace. The olive harvest is in full swing in late November and early December, bringing the farming year to an end. You would expect communities to hunker down in winter, but, as Carnival approaches, the whole island comes alive with age-old rituals that are unique to Sardinia, and Easter follows suit.

What to see

Beaches that compare with the best in the Caribbean would be reason enough

A bird's-eye view of roofs

A beautiful beach near Alghero – just one of the many on Sardinia

to venture here, but Sardinia has so much more. Dozens of medieval churches, thousands of ancient sites, age-old customs and colourful festivals; not to mention the delicious food and quaffable wine! It is a destination where you can fill a holiday itinerary two or three times over.

What to wear

Layering is the byword here. In summer, light cotton or breathable clothing is advisable for sightseeing. Take a long-sleeved item in case your arms and shoulders get sunburned, but the weather is so reliable that you should not need any cool weather clothing. Be aware that swimsuits and bikinis are not suitable attire for the towns and should be confined to the beaches; Italians like to sunbathe topless and this is rarely a problem even on the busiest of beaches.

Spring and autumn will be warm, so keep the light cotton outfits, but pack a couple of warmer layers (a fleece is ideal), especially for the fresher evenings. The island can be subject to spectacular storms, so a weatherproof jacket might be useful.

In the winter months, warm and waterproof clothing is advised though it certainly is not unusual to be able to wear T-shirts in December or January. The evenings, however, will be chilly.

For sightseeing do not forget to pack a pair of comfortable shoes.

Getting around
By bus

The bus services get to just about everywhere on Sardinia. The disadvantage is that they can be slow and infrequent, with several companies operating in different regions. The main pan-island company, Azienda Regionale Sarda Transporti or ARST (*tel: 800 865042; www.arst.sardegna.it*), runs bus services in many areas. These connect with Ferrovie Meridionali Sarde services (*tel: 800 044553; www.ferroviemeridionalisarde.it*) and Ferrovie della Sardegna (FdS) coaches (*tel: 070 342341; www.ferroviesardegna.it*).

By car

By far the best way to tour the island is by car. Your own vehicle allows you to get to the many deserted bays and out-of-the-way archaeological sites and churches, and it allows you to set the pace rather than a tour guide.

By train

Sardinia has a railway system covering over 1,000km (620 miles) of track. Lines run from Cágliari to Porto Torres via Oristano and Sassari, with branch lines to Iglesias and Carbonia, and to Olbia and to Alghero from Sassari. The system is run by TrenItalia, the state company, and you can buy a weekly tourist pass with unlimited travel, which includes travel on the Trenino Verde (*see below*). For more detail on services, consult *www.trenitalia.it*.

The Trenino Verde runs on 950mm (37-inch) narrow-gauge tracks and originally supplemented the standard-gauge lines in a few remote areas. Today this railway is one of Sardinia's unique tourist attractions: a chance to travel with ease through some of the island's most beautiful natural landscapes, and on a steam train to boot!

There are three lines: Macomer to Bosa, Mandas to Arbatax, and Ísili to Sorgono. The Trenino Verde runs in high summer only (July–August). For more information, *tel: 070 580246* or see *www.treninoverde.com* or *www.ferroviesardegna.it*.

See also Public Transport, *p188*.

The formalities

The Italian authorities still require that you register with the local police if you stay in one place for over three days. Hotels and campsites will do this for

A modern train at Iglesias station

Impressions

you, but you should look in at your local police station if you are in self-catering accommodation, unless you are sure that your hosts have registered you themselves.

Cultural traits
Watch out!
Sheep and cattle rustling has a long tradition and locals will tell you that it still goes on, so Sardinians have found a simple way to protect flocks. You may not see a human shepherd, but all flocks will have their guard dogs:

animals that live with sheep from an early age and believe that they are sheep. They will rest in the shade somewhere close, so do not approach the flocks when they are grazing because you may get a nasty surprise.

Cultural icons
On Sardinia you will find those little touches that have kept Italy on top in the style stakes: the cute Fiat Cinquecento cars zoom the streets, Vespa scooters weave among strollers in the pedestrian alleyways and chic

Religious products for sale

teenagers oozing cool grace street-corner cafés.

An independent spirit

Do not be surprised if you find farmers carrying firearms in the countryside. It is still common practice for farmers and shepherds to carry some kind of protection, and if they happen to spot a rabbit that would make a tasty meal – so much the better. Road signs also make popular targets, especially ones with the Italian as opposed to the Sardinian spelling of place names!

Siesta time

You will find that you get a lot more out of your trip if you set your body clock to Italian time when you arrive. Summers are extremely hot here, so the tradition of the siesta or afternoon rest was born to alleviate the need to toil during the hottest time of day.

On Sardinia, siesta is not just a couple of hours. Everything closes between noon and 1pm and very little opens again until 4pm. Where shops are concerned it is usually 5pm. You will find most cities and towns become deathly quiet in the mid-afternoons. If you do intend to carry on doing the tourist thing during the afternoon, please give a thought to people resting around you; loud conversations can be disturbing.

A little respect

Do remember that the churches you visit are places of worship to the

The Fiat Cinquecento is still to be found here

Sardinians. Take off hats and do not enter churches in beachwear. Ideally, women should cover their shoulders and men should wear a T-shirt or shirt and long trousers.

A common sight

One thing that might blight your trip is the amount of litter you will see in the countryside. Sadly, drivers are quite happy to throw paper and packets out of windows as they drive along and hedgerows are awash with abandoned material. It is the only blot on an otherwise naturally pristine landscape.

SMOKING

In 2004 the Italian authorities banned smoking in all public places – which makes restaurants and cafés a much more inviting prospect for visitors who do not enjoy the 'pastime' of passive smoking.

Cágliari

*'There was a certain pleasant, natural robustness
of spirit, and something of a feudal
free-and-easiness.'*

D H LAWRENCE
Sea and Sardinia

Much of Lawrence's description still holds true today. Sardinia's capital, pronounced Calyari, is a likeable city, full of street life and style but not constantly gazing in the mirror as if in love with itself, as some Italian cities seem to do.

The active university brings a youthful feel, but even the historic heart is replete with family homes, so kids play and old people while away the hours chatting.

The old city is divided into several distinct districts, making sightseeing relatively easy. Each of these has a different atmosphere, from the historic castle to the residential quarters, with their lines of drying clothes festooned like bunting across the narrow alleys. The city is surrounded by fantastic beaches and vast salt flats that are a birdwatcher's delight.

Castello

Castello, as the name suggests, is the fortified inner sanctum that sits on the high ground, dominating the rest of the city. The first major defensive structures were built by the Pisans in the early 13th century. These were expanded and reinforced by the Aragonese, Spanish and Piedmontese. Castello has always been the administrative heart of the town and even today hosts Sardinia's governmental institutions. You will find the cathedral here, and lots of art and antiques shops set among the fine, but sometimes careworn, baroque and neoclassical townhouses. In the heart of the quarter, the Citadel Museo, are four of the city's major museums.

This area was badly damaged during World War II, resulting in the few open spaces that now exist, some of which have been landscaped to produce airy spots in which to relax.

Marina

Lying between the waterfront and the southern walls of Castello, Marina is a lively district full of small bars and eaties, from cheap and cheerful trattoria to fine restaurants. The façade that faces the water is an elegant ensemble of neoclassical five- and six-storey buildings, with an arcade at ground level housing atmospheric cafés, souvenir emporia and news kiosks where you can buy foreign papers.

This part of the city was founded in Punic times and has always been the trading district. It was the gritty workaday quarter where the sailors would spend their hard-earned cash on booze and women, where deals were done for spices and customs officials collected their taxes.

Stampace

West of Castello and Marina, Stampace (pronounced Stampechey) also reaches the waterfront, where you will find the ornate confection that is Cágliari Municipio (Town Hall), rebuilt in every overblown detail after damage in 1943. This is the oldest residential district in the city, with a tight maze of streets offering fascinating corners. By

Cágliari

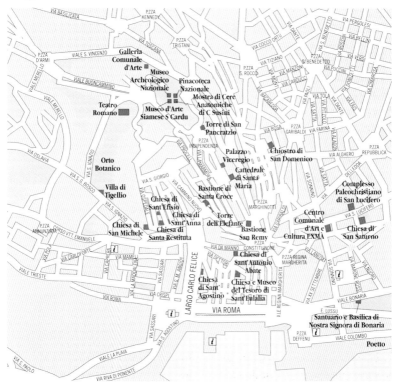

contrast, it has the capital's largest green space, the Botanical Garden.

Largo Carlo Felice separates Marina and Stampace, and the two areas are connected by Piazza Yenne, with its numerous bars and cafés. This busy square is crowned by a statue of King Carlo Felice dressed as a Roman Caesar. Below this is the marked starting point of the Cágliari to Porto Torres or Carlo Felice road, the Viceroy's crowning achievement.

Villanova

Spreading north and east of the old core, Villanova derives its name from the spread of the town west of the Pisan citadel in medieval times, and rapid expansion during the Spanish era.

A district of wider streets, lined with apartment blocks, it has fewer tourist attractions, but the few that are there are worth the visit.

WHAT TO SEE
Bastione di Santa Croce (Holy Cross Bastion)

The tower protecting the approaches to the upper Castello district was a secondary defence built by the Pisans. *Castello.*

Bastione San Remy (St Remy Bastion)

The most impressive element in the 18th-century restructuring of the Castello city walls, the bastion was erected as the southeast lookout. Today, a large open square has been

incorporated into the design, and from here there are good views across the city. It is also a meeting point for young skateboarders who can act as a disconcerting mobile obstacle course! Two sets of monumental stone staircases built in the early 19th century lead down to Piazza Constituzione and into the Marina district below. *Castello.*

Cattedrale di Santa Maria (Duomo)

The core of this church is 13th-century Pisan but it has been extended several times, including an upgrade in the 17th century and a controversial facelift in the form of a neo-Gothic façade in the 1930s. Historians are outraged at the audacity of the Mussolini regime at what they claim is a defiling of this historic building, but after 70 years the stone has mellowed and does not look much out of place.

The interior is ornate baroque but contains some exceptional late 13th-century objects, including a large pulpit gifted to the city by the Pisans. It has now been split into two and separated

Painted detail in Cágliari Cathedral

Bastione San Remy

from the four huge carved lions representing the four evangelists that it once supported.

Next door to the Duomo is the Curia Arcivescovile (Archbishop's Palace), built at the same time as the church in the 13th century. It was also renovated in the 17th century, resulting in its rather stern baroque façade.

Piazza Palazzo (Castello).
Open: 8am–12.30pm & 4.30–8pm.

Centro Comunale d'Art e Cultura EXMÀ (EXMÀ Cultural and Art Centre)

The name EXMÀ comes from *ex-mattatoio* because the building used to be the *mattatoio* or municipal slaughterhouse from 1845 until 1964. In the 1990s the city of Cágliari turned it into a cultural centre and it now hosts temporary exhibitions, with everything from folk art to photography and computer-generated images.

Via San Lucifero 71 (modern town).
Tel: 070 666399. Open: June–Sept Tue–Sat 10am–1pm & 5–10pm; Oct–May Tue–Sat 10am–1pm & 4–8pm. Admission charge.

Chiesa di Sant'Agostino (Church of St Augustine)

The ancient convent of St Augustine was demolished to make way for a reorganisation of fortifications in the Marina quarter in the 16th century. Construction on this new church began in 1577 and it is the only example of Renaissance architecture in the city. Recent excavations below ground level have revealed yet more Roman remains and the church is currently closed to allow these to continue.

Via Baylle. Largo Carlo Felice (Marina).

Chiesa di Sant'Anna

Chiesa di Sant'Anna
(Church of St Anne)

The fine baroque façade of Sant'Anna dominates its tiny square, but at least you have space to stand back and admire the lines, unlike some other churches on the island. The church was bombed in 1943, so the building you see today is a faithful recreation.
Piazza Santa Restituta (Stampace). Open: daily 10am–1pm & 5–7pm.

Chiesa di Sant'Antonio Abate
(Church of St Anthony)

Tightly packed into the cluster of streets in the northern Marina, this church could be easily passed but it has a fascinating history. It was part of a larger site of a medieval hospital complex run by the Hospitallers of Saint Anthony of Vienne that was founded in 1360. The whole complex was refurbished in the 1630s during a massive expansion of the city defences planned by Fra'Just.
Via Manno (Marina). Open: for services only.

Chiesa di San Michele
(Church of St Michael)

The baroque excess of the façade masks an unusual entrance. Once through the stone arches, you turn right up a short flight of stairs to enter the church. The architects have made something special out of an unpromising locale when viewed from Via Azuni – the street to the church from Piazza Yenne – as the façade fills the space between the houses on either side.

Charles V visited here on one of his political campaigns, keeping the disparate elements of his vast empire on his side. The stone pulpit that graces the outer atrium is named after him, but the rococo interior is the *pièce de résistance*, with the colourful frescoes set off by acres of gold leaf.
Via Ospedale (Stampace). Open: daily 8am–noon & 6–8.30pm.

Chiesa di Sant'Efisio
(Church of St Efisio)

Built to honour Cágliari's patron saint on the site where he was imprisoned before his martyr's death at Nora (*see pp63–4*) in AD 303, the Church of Sant'Efisio sees mass celebrations during the feast day on 1 May.

Erected in the last two decades of the 1700s on the site of an older smaller

THE SANT'EFISIO CELEBRATIONS

In 1652 Cágliari was in the midst of a devastating plague that threatened to decimate the population. The townsfolk prayed to their patron saint and 'miraculously' the pestilence ceased. So on 1 May each year the whole of Cágliari recreates the fateful final journey Bishop Efisio made to Nora, where he met his death. At the head of the solemn procession south out of the city is the 17th-century statue of the saint set in a magnificent coach and following behind are hundreds of Sardinians dressed in elaborate traditional costumes.

The day has become the biggest folk festival on the island calendar.

ground plan seen today. It fell into disuse as early as the medieval era and was partly dismantled in 1699, when some of the stone was recycled. Damaged in World War II, the site was closed from 1978 until 1996 but has since been made safe. Modern glass walls were added to create an architecturally interesting exhibition area.

Piazza San Cosimo (modern town). Open: Tue–Sat 10am–1pm & 3.30–7.30pm. Admission charge.

church, the restrained façade hides a wealth of baroque decoration.

A small subterranean chamber underneath the present church has been identified, but not definitely verified, as the cell where Bishop Efisio spent his last days. Other excavations have uncovered human remains dating back to the 1st century AD and the architectural elements of what appears to be a Roman temple.

Via Sant'Efisio (Stampace). Open: Tue–Sun 9am–1pm & 4–7pm.

Chiesa di San Saturno (Church of St Saturno)

The finest paleo-Christian basilica in the city is built on the site where Saturno was beheaded in AD 304 on the orders of Roman Emperor Diocletian (*see p51*). The site was put under the auspices of the Benedictines in 1089 and extended to create the cruciform

Chiesa di Sant'Antonio Abate

Chiesa di Santa Restituta, one of the most important religious buildings in Cágliari

Chiesa e Museo del Tesoro e Area Archeologico di Sant'Eulalia (Church of St Eulalia, the Museum of Liturgical Treasures and Archaeological Area)

Built in the 14th century in Catalan-Gothic style, the church would be a side attraction were it not for its liturgical treasures and the discoveries made here during excavations in the 1990s. The chance finding of an ancient well led to a full-scale investigation of what lay underneath the church and a whole 'world under a world', the streets of Roman Karales, was revealed. The entire quarter was thought to have been filled in during the 6th century in a remodelling attempt. The church preserves some valuable religious artefacts, including vestments, gold and silverware, plus rare medieval documents and books.

Vico del Collegio 2 (Marina). Tel: 070 663724. Open: Oct–June Tue–Sat 10am–1pm & 5–8pm; July–Sept daily 10am–1pm & 4–9pm. Admission charge.

Chiostro di San Domenico (The Dominican Cloister)

In 1254, the Dominicans began a vast monasterial complex just outside the city walls. Three hundred years later, in the 16th century, the order razed the structure and invested in a 'modern' development in Catalan-Gothic style that was to become the Sardinian headquarters for the Spanish Inquisition during those years of terror. The monastery remained pretty much intact until the 19th century, but the cloister and crypt are all that remains today. The cloister is one of the finest examples of monumental religious architecture on Sardinia and it is worth spending a little time taking in the fine detail of the carving here.

Via XXIV Maggio (Villanova).
Open: Tue–Sun 9am–1pm &
4.30–7.30pm. Admission charge.

Complesso Paleochristiano di San Lucifero (Paleo-Christian Complex of St Lucifer)

The baroque shell of San Lucifero hides the remnants of a much more interesting paleo-Christian edifice dating back to the 6th century. The tiny church is said to contain the bones of Bishop Lucifero.

Via San Lucifero (modern town).
Open: daily 9am–1pm & 4.30–8pm.

Chiesa di Santa Restituta (Church of St Restituta)

One of the most revered religious buildings in Cágliari, the present Santa Restituta was built in the 1630s on top of the paleo-Christian crypt said to house the remains of Restituta, martyred during the 4th century. Facts on the woman are a little vague, but she may have been the mother of Bishop Eusabio. This early church was used by the Byzantines and continued to be an active place of worship for the Orthodox Christian community until the 13th century. The site was excavated by the Catholic establishment during the Counter-Reformation, and the human bones discovered here were proclaimed Restituta's by the papacy.

The church was used as a bomb shelter during World War II and was left in ruins until further excavations were carried out in the 1970s. These brought Roman and pre-Roman remains to light, adding weight to claims that this was once a pagan place of worship.

Via Sant'Efisio (Stampace).
Open: daily 9am–1pm & 4–7pm.

Galleria Comunale d'Arte (Cágliari City Art Gallery)

Often forgotten in the rush to get the national collections crossed off the 'seen' list, Cágliari's city art gallery is worth a visit. There is a fine collection of 19th- and 20th-century Italian art and 20th-century Sardinian art, including a vast donation by Francesco Paolo Ingrao (1909–99), and also

The Church of Saint Eulalia built in the Catalan-Gothic style

Cágliari

contrasting galleries of Romanesque works from the 9th and 10th centuries. *Giardini Pubblici, Largo Giuseppe Dessì. (Castello). Tel: 070 490727. Open: summer Wed–Mon 9am–1pm & 5–9pm; winter Wed–Mon 9am–1pm & 3.30–7.30pm. Admission charge.*

Museo Archeologico Nazionale (National Archaeological Museum)

The finest and most comprehensive archaeological collection on the island, the National Museum is housed in a state-of-the-art renovation of part of the old citadel. Finds from every corner have been brought together in a journey through Sardinia's complicated ancient history, starting with Neolithic remains, including flint arrowheads and votive statuettes, discovered in the Sirri/Carbonia region.

The artefacts of the Nuraghic peoples shed great light on their sophistication, and the museum has an excellent collection of *bronzetti*, the small metal figurines that are the singular most impressive relic of Nuraghic artistry. They were produced on many different themes and depict warriors, sportsmen, domestic animals and ships. Other collections include ceramics and weapons and a series of model *nuraghi*, that archaeologists think formed a basis of cult worship.

The Phoenician era presented some excellent finds from the cities at Monte Sirai, Nora, Sulcis and Tharros, including funerary artefacts such as carved stelae,

A statue in the Museo Archeologico Nazionale, dating from c. 8th century BC

objects for ritual purification and terracotta urns. Look for the carved stele from Nora, where the name Shrdn, the precursor of Sardinia, was first written.

While the lower galleries provide a chronological understanding, the upper exhibition halls offer a geographical tour of the major sites, allowing you to plan an itinerary of those you consider most important and relevant.

Moving on from the pre-Classical world, the museum has a fine collection of Roman artefacts with monumental statuary and excellent mosaics, and the timeline leads on to the medieval era. *Cittadella dei Musei, Piazza Arsenale (Castello). Tel: 070 655911. Open: Tue–Sun 9am–7.30pm. Admission charge, combined ticket with the Pinacoteca Nazionale (see pp46–8).*

Museo d'Arte Siamese S Cardu (Museum of Siamese Arts S Cardu)

Local boy made good Stefano Cardu (1849–1933) spent over twenty years working in what we now call Thailand (in those days, Siam) as builder to the king. It is even said that he built the royal palace in Bangkok. Cardu returned to Cágliari with a boatload of Asian artworks that are now one of the most important collections of their kind in Europe. He donated his vast 1,300-piece collection to the city and it went on show to the public in 1923.

Cardu collected beautiful objects without regard for their purpose, so along with incredibly ornate and intricate hand-carved religious statues you have domestic ware of elegant simplicity and fine weaponry. Carved ivory, rare hardwoods and precious metals are some of the materials used, and you also find Ming and Qing dynasty Chinese porcelain.

Cittadella dei Musei, Piazza Arsenale (Castello). Tel: 070 651888. Open: summer Tue–Sun 9am–1pm & 4–8pm; winter Tue–Sun 9am–1pm & 3.30–7.30pm. Admission charge.

A display at the National Archaeological Museum

Mostra di Cere Anatomiche di C Susini (Collection of Anatomical Waxworks)

In the early 19th century the science of surgery was in its infancy and even a surgeon's understanding of how the human body works was limited. The only way to increase understanding was to perform dissections on dead bodies, but there were not enough of these for the anatomy classes that were springing up all across Europe. In 1801 Professor Francesco Antonio Boi left Cágliari to improve his knowledge of anatomy by studying under the eminent Professor Paolo Mascani, and during his time here he contracted Clemente Susini to create wax models of the cadavers he was dissecting. These are some of the most accurate and realistic wax models of their kind and were completed in 1805. The models were immediately bought by the Sardinian Viceroy Carlo Felice for his private Museum of Antiquities and Natural History. Later, they became the property of the university and were put on display at their new permanent home in 1991.

The models are not for the faint-hearted and show graphic details of the torso and intestines, heads without flesh, and muscles and tendons attached to the bone.

Cittadella dei Musei, Piazza Arsenale (Castello). Tel: 070 664783.
Open: Tue–Sun 9am–1pm & 5–9pm.
Admission charge.

Orto Botanico (Botanical Garden)

Cágliari's 'green lung' sits in the west of the Stampace district. The park covers five hectares (12^1/$_2$ acres) and has over 1,000 species of trees and other plants from all around the world. Scattered around are remains of the Punic and Roman city. To the north of the garden is the Roman Amphitheatre (*see p48*), and close by to the south are the remains of the Roman Villa di Tigellio.

Via Sant'Ignazio da Láconi 13 (Stampace). Tel: 070 6753522.
Open: daily 8am–1.30pm & 3–7pm.
Admission charge.
Villa di Tigellio, Via Tigellio (Stampace).
Open: Mon–Fri 9am–1pm.
Admission charge.

Palazzo Viceregio or Palazzo Regio (Viceroy's Palace)

The Palazzo Viceregio has been the administrative heart of the island since 1885. Built on the site of the first Pisan fort, the core of the building is early 15th-century Catalan, but it was given a grand makeover to house the legislature. It has recently gone through another renovation process to restore disparate elements. Today it houses the Prefettura or Sardinian Provincial Assembly.

Piazza Palazzo (Castello).
Not open to the public.

Pinacoteca Nazionale (National Art Gallery)

Housed in the old Arsenal, the museum was inaugurated in its present building

A path in Cágliari's Botanical Garden

in 1992. The main collection centres on religious art rescued from churches around the island, particularly the Catalan-Gothic retables (a frame or shelf enclosing decorated panels or revered objects that sat behind the main altar) that date from the 14th- to 16th-century Spanish period, including pieces by named Catalan artists J Mates (1391–1431), J Barcelo (*c.* 1488–1516), Joan Figuera (1455–79) and the enigmatic Maestro di Castelsardo.

The pieces of the Maestro di Sanluri, painted at the beginning of the 16th century, show the influence of Italian styles that gradually supplanted the Catalan style. During this period there was a thriving artistic movement that came to be known as the School of Stampace. The leading light was Pietro Cavaro, who has four works on display, dating from 1520–25.

There is also a good ethnographic collection featuring Sardinian textiles, filigree and other traditional jewellery, ceramics and weapons.

Complesso Cittadella dei Musei (Castello). Tel: 070 674054. Open: Tue–Sun 9am–8pm. Admission charge, combined with Museo Archeologico Nazionale (see p44).

Teatro Romano (Roman Amphitheatre)

The largest single remaining monument of the Roman era on the island, the amphitheatre is 2nd century AD. The *cavea* (seating area) is cut out of a natural cleft in the rock and is well preserved. Audiences still attend concerts held throughout summer.

Viale Fra'Ignazio (Stampace). Open: daily 10am–4pm. Admission charge.

Torre dell'Elefante (Elephant Tower)

One of the original towers set in the Pisan Castello walls, the Torre

Sardinia has the only Roman amphitheatre in the world that has been carved out of the rock

dell'Elefante guarded the approach from Stampace to the west. The design reveals a great deal about defensive structures of the time, with strong, plain walls on three sides and a simple wooden stairway that was open on the Castello side. It is thought that the Pisans did not see the logic of having a wall on the inside since they only needed to defend the outer facing structure.

The crenellated top floor was a 19th-century addition and was used to house political prisoners. Today, the tower, named after the tiny carved elephant that graces the outer wall, offers wonderful views over the red-tiled roofs of the city.

Via Università (Castello). Open: Apr–Oct Tue–Sun 9am–1pm & 3.30–7.30pm; Nov–Mar Tue–Sun 9am–5pm. Admission free.

Detail on the Elephant Tower

Torre di San Pancratzio (Tower of St Pancreas)

A sister tower to Torre dell'Elefante, the Torre di San Pancratzio sits on the eastern wall as you leave the Arsenal, overlooking the sea. Built by the Pisans in 1305, the open stairwell was walled in to create a solid structure and it was then used as a storehouse and later the Castello prison. Today, it has been renovated to the original medieval plan.

Piazza Indipendenza (Castello). Open: Apr–Oct Tue–Sun 9am–1pm & 3.30–7.30pm; Nov–Mar Tue–Sun 9am–5pm. Admission free.

OUTSIDE CÁGLIARI
Castello di San Michele (St Michael's Castle)

The capital's newest exhibition and cultural centre was once a major defence sitting on high ground behind the modern city, with views over land to the north and the sea to the south. The castle was built in the late Byzantine, early Giudicato era at the end of the first millennium. It was the home of the powerful Carroz family until the 16th century, when it passed to the Spanish crown, who used it as a plague hospital. In 1895 it was bought and renovated by Roberto di San Tomossso but was commandeered by Italian forces in the 1930s. A grand

Ruins of the tower of Poetto

conversion process was completed just after the 2000 millennium.

Colle di San Michele (close to the Nuovo Ospedale Civile). Tel: 070 500656. Open: Tue–Sun 10am–1pm & 5–8pm. Admission charge.

Poetto

Cágliari's beaches would make any city proud. Four kilometres (2½ miles) of fine wide sand are backed with ample trendy bars and cafés that lie just a five-minute drive from the city. Of course the locals make ample use of the resource just on their doorstep, and summer days and spring and autumn weekends see the huge crowds arriving for sun and fun. It is a fantastic place to people watch while sunbathing.

Behind the beach, the Stagno di Molentargius is a vast salt flat that is an important resting place for flamingoes in the spring and autumn.

Santuario e Basilica di Nostra Signora di Bonaria (Sanctuary and Basilica of Our Lady of Bonaria)

A short walk out of the old town and overlooking the port, the sanctuary is the only remaining part of a fortress built by the Catalans. Its patron is a protector of mariners. Sailors from around the world called in, and some still do, when they docked at Cágliari's port. Their ex-voto objects can be found in a small museum in the interior. The wooden statue at the heart of the complex is an object of veneration and was washed into the harbour in a wooden crate in 1370.

The blousy big sister to the sanctuary, the Basilica, was started in the first decade of the 19th century but took over a hundred years to complete. *Viale Bonaria. Open: daily 6.30am–noon & 4.30–7.30pm.*

The Basilica di Bonaria took over a hundred years to build

DIOCLETIAN'S RULE

The reign of Gaius Aurelius Valerius Diocletianus proved to be one of the most interesting in the late Roman era. He brought to a decisive end what is now known as the Imperial Crisis, but is remembered with disdain by the Church for his brutal treatment of the early Christians.

Born circa AD 245 on the Dalmatian coast of what is now Croatia, to a very humble family, Diocletian used a career in the army to improve his own personal standing. He moved through many positions of influence, gaining the then emperor's eye. By the 280s he was in control, but Rome was awash with disparate armies and he had to secure increasingly fragile borders.

Diocletian bolstered the religious imperial cult, identifying himself with the Roman god Jupiter. This may initially have been an exercise in public relations to strengthen the image of the empire in the minds of his citizens, because he was lenient with other religions. However, over time, his policies grew increasingly severe. Even though it is thought his wife and daughter were Christians, all faiths other than the Imperial cult were banned in 303 and many prominent Christians put to brutal death, including Bishop Efisio (*see pp40–41*) and Saturno. Many of these individuals are now canonised, beatified or revered as martyrs. This was the last, but greatest persecution of Christians of the Roman Empire, with more than 3,000 put to death.

Walk: Cágliari

With a pair of comfortable shoes, Cágliari is the perfect place to explore on foot. In addition to interesting major attractions there is a wealth of domestic architecture to enjoy, shops to browse in and café tables where you can take time to watch the world come to you.

Time: 4 hours.

Distance: 3km (1¾ miles)

Leave the car in one of the parking spaces between the waterfront and the Marina district and find Largo Carlo Felice, the wide boulevard that runs from the port into the heart of the old town. On the right-hand side, about 300m (330yds) along the route, you will find the following places:

1 Chiesa di Sant'Agostino

This is a Renaissance building erected in 1577 but currently closed to allow archaeologists to excavate Roman remains found under the church floor.
Continue walking along Largo Carlo Felice. Cross the street when you reach Piazza Yenne (with the statue of Carlo Felice dressed in a Roman tunic) and continue walking past the statue, turning left at the top of the square along Via Azuni. Directly ahead you will see the façade of Chiesa di San Michele.

2 Chiesa di San Michele

The interior is a rococo masterpiece.
Walk back along Via Azuni and take the fourth alley on the left to Chiesa di Sant'Efisio.

3 Chiesa di Sant'Efisio

This church is dedicated to the island's patron saint and houses a revered statue.
From Sant'Efisio walk back towards Via Azuni, then take the alleyway on the right to Chiesa di Santa Restituta.

4 Chiesa di Santa Restituta

The crypt was a pagan temple taken over by early Christians. It was used as a bomb shelter during World War II.
Return to Via Azuni in the direction of Piazza Yenne, where you will see Chiesa di Sant'Anna.

5 Chiesa di Sant'Anna

This is one of the finest religious façades in the city.
Return to Piazza Yenne and make your way up the narrow alley at the top right-hand side of the square. This leads to a free lift that takes you into the citadel.

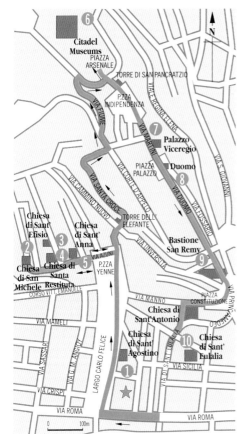

Leave Arsenale and walk straight ahead into the greater Castello area and into Piazza Indipendenza, where you will find Torre di San Pancratzio on the left. Carry on to the Palazzo Viceregio.

7 Palazzo Viceregio

This 18th-century palazzo has a 15th-century core. It now houses the Sardinian Provincial Assembly.
Continue walking past the palazzo and you will reach the Duomo after 200m (220yds).

8 The Duomo

The Duomo has a 1930s façade but houses important Gothic decoration.
Continue on down Via Duomo and you will eventually reach Bastione San Remy.

9 Bastione San Remy

This monumental restructuring of the city walls in the 18th century is one of the best vantage points for visitors.
Take the ornate stairway down to Piazza Constituzione, passing out of the Castello quarter into the Marina district. Turn right along Via Manno and left at Chiesa di Sant'Antonio. Then walk along Via di Sant'Eulalia, where you will find the church on the left.

10 Chiesa di Sant'Eulalia

Enjoy the Roman remains and the liturgical treasures at the museum.

Turn left out of the lift and walk along the city walls past Torre dell'Elefante on the left and along Via Santa Croce. Keep climbing until the entrance to the citadel comes into view on the right. Once through the gate, turn left into the Arsenale area.

6 Citadel Museums

Here you will find four museums, and you will certainly not want to miss the archaeological collection.

The south

The swathe of land around Cágliari holds a fascinating melange of attractions from great Roman cities to hilltop parks. Its major beaches are splendid but well known to the capital's population, so they are often busier than others around the island and a great place to watch Italian youth at play (such as Chia), or are combined with atmospheric fishing ports (such as Porto Pino west of Teulada). The southwestern countryside has long been Sardinia's most industrial area.

The mines worked during Phoenician and Roman times were reopened in the 19th century and again during Mussolini's drive for self-sufficiency in the 1930s. You will also be able to explore the history of the south's most famous feudal Giudice, Ugolino della Gherardesca, made famous by Dante in his *Inferno*, which documents Ugolino's Machiavellian machinations and his violent death.

Buggeru

This small resort has developed a reputation as a laid-back surf centre, where the young crowd gather during the off-season. The Henry Road above the town is now a footpath, offering extensive views along the coast. It was once the road from the inland mines to the loading docks in the bay. The cliffscapes here are spectacular.

Capo Carbonara (Cape Carbonara)

Capo Carbonara is Sardinia's southeastern tip. In 1998 the Capo Carbonara Protected Marine Area was established to protect over 9,000 hectares (22,200 acres) of coastal waters around the cape, where the water quality offers an excellent environment for sea flora and marine creatures of all kinds. The protection extends to Stagno Notteri, which is a worthwhile and generally deserted (by humans) flamingo resting spot, so it makes for excellent birdwatching.

On your journey you will find a Catalan castle, **Fortezza Vecchia**, that has been renovated and opened as a small archaeological museum plus exhibition about pirates and their history on the island. Spiaggia del Simius is a lovely place for a stroll for an hour or so in the surf. The tip of the cape is reached by a footpath.
Fortezza Vecchia: south of Villasimius. Tel: 070 7930232. Open: mid-June–mid-Sept daily 10am–1pm & 6–9pm; mid-Sept–mid-June Fri–Sun 10am–1pm & 6–9pm. Admission charge.

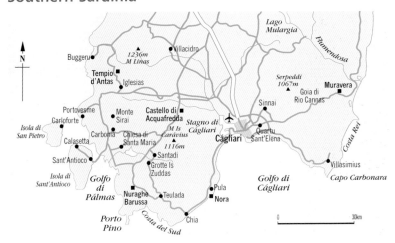

Carbonia

Founded in the 1930s when Mussolini invested in the mining industry, Carbonia (yes, the reason for the name really is that obvious) is a rather nondescript town though lovers of modernist architecture might want to take a side trip for the Chiesa di San Ponziano. It is also worth a detour to visit the two major museum collections.

Museo Archeologico di Villa Sulcis (Sulcis Archaeological Museum) displays artefacts excavated at the ancient Phoenician site of Sulcis close by and in the city and necropolis on Monte Sirai (*see p62*). The museum holds workshops on traditional crafts including ceramics during the summer.

Museo Speleo E A Martel (Palaeontology and Speleology Museum) is the only one of its kind in Sardinia. The galleries have fascinating fossils and bones, including the eggs of a philoceratops, the claws of a Tyrannosaurus rex and woolly mammoth bones. The museum acts as a centre for information on archaeological and environmental issues.

Museo Archeologico di Villa Sulcis: Via Napoli 4. Tel: 0781 691131. Open: Tue–Sun 9am–1pm & 3–7pm. Admission charge.

Museo Speleo E A Martel: Via Campania 61/b. Tel: 0781 691006. Open: June–Sept daily 9am–1pm & 4–8pm; Oct–May daily 9am–1pm & 3–7pm. Admission charge.

Castello di Acquafredda (Acquafredda Castle)

The walls of Castello di Acquafredda, set high on its volcanic 'plug', seem to be an extension of the living rock. The castle was erected in the early 13th century when the Pisans decided to protect their mining operations to the south. This vantage point controlled the vast plain to the north and the pass through the hills to the west. The castle belonged to the della Gherardesca clan during their suzerainty of the region. *South of Siliqua. Open access. Free admission.*

Chia

One of the longest and best beaches in southern Sardinia and a popular place for sun worshippers, windsurfers and surfers. In summer it is a place to see and be seen in, so bring your fashionable beachwear. Behind the extensive dunes are brackish marshlands to explore.

Chiesa di Santa Maria

The small stone village of Tratalias was abandoned in the 1950s when water from the nearby reservoir began to undermine the foundations, but today life is slowly returning as the soil stabilises. At the heart of this rather scruffy semi-ghost town is a little gem, the late Romanesque Church of Santa Maria, founded in 1213, and a fine example of restrained architecture both inside and out. The church was the cathedral of the surrounding diocese until the seat was moved to Iglesias (*see pp59–60*) in 1503. The rather curious set of stone steps on the pediment at the top of the façade is typical of Pisan design, along with the

Fishing boats near Chia

two lozenge bas-relief carvings on either side of the door. If the church is closed, cross the square to the café for information.
Tratalias. Not open regular hours. Donations accepted.

Costa del Sud

One of the prettiest coastal routes on the island, the Costa del Sud comprises rolling hills and sandy bays that invite you to stop for a spot of swimming and snorkelling. In the east the coast is bounded by the beach and resort of Chia, while the fledgling port of Porto di Teulada, whose inland town Teulada hosts an annual Sculpture Festival in early September, marks the western border. Virtually every corner offers vertiginous views down to emerald waters or panoramas across sandy bays.

The southernmost point of the coast, Capo Spartivento, sports a modern lighthouse, and a little further west there is a Catalan tower at Capo Malfanato. *South of Teulada.*

Costa Rei

The southeasternmost coastal bays of Sardinia offer some enticing and less visited beaches and a wonderful route up the east coast into the Gennargentu.

The Costa Rei has been compared by some to the Costa Smeralda (*see pp130–33*), and in many ways it has some credence because Costa Rei is also characterised by dramatic rock formations, though the rocks of the Smeralda are much more red than the rocks here, which take on a sand/golden hue. The Rei, however, has far more sand than the Smeralda, and many more fine strands that are undeveloped.

The costa is bounded by the Bay of Sant'Elmo to the south and the Bay of Capo Ferrato in the north, a stretch of around 15km (9¹/₂ miles) that, in addition to exquisite beaches, also has several small marshes, wonderful places to study native and migratory wildlife.

Goia di Rio Cannas

The inland route northeast of Cágliari to Arbatax leads through the attractive valley of the River Cannas. On either

The Costa del Sud is ideal for swimming

side are peaks reaching over 500m (1,640ft), including the Park of the Sette Fratelli (Seven Brothers), where you can enjoy Mediterranean woodland, waterfalls and sculpture on the slopes of one of the highest peaks in the southeast at over 1,000m (3,280ft). There is also Monte Minni Minni, where trails lead through stands of ancient pine and oak to the summit at just over 700m (2,295ft), with views to the Seven Brothers to the west, and down to the white sand beaches of Villasimius to the south.

Grotte Is Zuddas

Said to be some of the oldest documented grottos in the world at 600 million years and certainly one of the largest on the island, the Grotte Is Zuddas display a spectacular array of huge stalactites and stalagmites but are most famed for rare crystal formations called helictites. The scientific

A view over Iglesias

description is that helictites are speleothems (mineral deposits in a cave, formed by the action of water) that change axis during their growth, giving an angular or curved shape. Scientists do not know for certain how they are formed, but one theory is that wind direction in the cave could play a part in altering the formation pattern.

Santadi holds a fascinating Matrimonio Maureddino or Moorish Wedding festival, on the first Sunday in August, when one couple from the area are married in full traditional costume, with all the trimmings. The town then spends the rest of the day in party mode.

5km (3 miles) south of Santadi.
Tel: 0781 955741. Open: Apr–Sept daily
9.30am–noon & 2.30–6pm; Oct–Mar
Mon–Fri noon–4.30pm, Sat & Sun
9.30am–noon & 2.30–4.30pm.
Admission charge.

Iglesias

The largest settlement in the southwest, Iglesias was renamed by the Spanish, who did not want to stick with Villa di Chiesa, the old Pisan epithet. The region was an important centre of mining even in Roman times – they called it Metalla. Today the suburbs are surrounded by extensive 19th- and 20th-century mine workings, the skeletons of their pithead factories and villages a testimony to a once very profitable industry that supported the town until the late 20th century. Some

might find these ugly, but the monotone grey hues lend a drama that is quite pleasing on the eye.

The centre of the old town offers a more mainstream attraction: a maze of narrow alleyways punctuated by small piazzas. There is a definite Catalan feel to the place, with lots of wrought-iron balconies overflowing with geraniums and bougainvillea. However, some of the most important buildings date to before Spanish rule, including the **Cattedrale di Santa Chiara**, which was commissioned by Ugolino della Gherardesca and finished in 1284. The façade is typically understated Pisan Romanesque, but the interior received a Catalan update in the 16th century. Across the square is the Municipio, a fine neoclassical edifice that is the administrative heart of the town today.

Ugolino gave the town a hint of self-rule in a series of codices called *Breve di Villa di Chiesa*, a copy of which can be seen in the town's historical archives, which ushered in a 'golden age'. The town housed a Pisan mint and sat within tall, impressive walls. The town returns to medieval garb for its major festival, commemorating its feudal past on 13 August each year, and on the 15th there is a candle ceremony, again dating back several hundred years.

If you want to know more about Iglesias' mining heritage, take a trip to the **Museo dell'Arte Minerale** (Museum of the Art of Minerals), once the school of mining and today a 'mine' of information about the methodology and theory of tunnelling. You can even find some practice tunnels dug by the apprentices that show different theories in action. You can visit some of the mine workings around the town but these are by guided tour only. Visit the tourist office to see if there are any in English. The **Grotta di Santa Barbara** is worth a visit. This huge crystal-encrusted cavern was discovered by accident in the 1950s when a new tunnel was being cut at the San Giovanni Mine.

Tourist office: Via Gramsci 11.
Tel: 0781 41795 (contact tourist office to book tours of the mines and the Grotta di Santa Barbara).
Cattedrale di Santa Chiara: Piazza del Municipio. Open: daily 8am–noon & 3.30–7pm. Admission free.
Museo dell'Arte Minerale: Via Roma 9. Tel: 0781 22304. Erratic opening times, calling ahead advised. Admission free.

Isola di San Pietro

This smaller sibling of Isola di Sant'Antioco (*see pp61–2*) was well populated in Nuraghic, Carthaginian and Roman times, when the island was known as Accipitrum Insula because of its large population of birds of prey. A modern population did not settle here, however, until the late 18th century, when Ligurian (mainland Italian) peoples, who had emigrated to the island of Tabarka just off the Tunisian coast, were forced to leave their home by the increased French presence along the North African coast and were given permission to start a new life here.

The first arrivals founded Carloforte, named after King Carlo Emanuele III, the then King of Sardinia. It was the only town on the island and a pretty settlement of pastel-coloured buildings. Now, as then, it makes its primary living from fishing and its tuna is famed around the world.

The town's **Museo Civico** (Civic Museum), set in the old fort, makes a good job of charting the history and economic development of the community. There is a room devoted to the tuna industry, exhibiting tools used in the *mattanza* (*see box below*), while another tells the story of the founding of the town through official documents loaned by the Italian state.

The rest of the island has only the occasional farmhouse or hamlet. La Punta, to the north of Carloforte, is the

THE *MATTANZA*

One of the strongest traditions on the island is the *mattanza* or slaughter, the much-anticipated tuna harvest that provides the fishing industry with much of its annual income.

When the fish arrive on well-known routes during their annual migration, an elaborate set of nets funnels them into the *camera della morte*, literally the 'death rooms,' where the fishermen pull out individuals, which can weigh over 100kg (15 stone) each, and club them to death. It is a bloody frenzy, which has attracted the attention of animal rights activists but no one has yet come up with a less violent method of satisfying the appetites of fish-eaters.

scene of the *mattanza* in May or early June. To the south you will be able to walk to the basalt column cliffs at Punta di Colonne (*tourist office: Corso Tagliafico 2, Carloforte. Tel: 0781 854009; www.prolococarloforte.it*).

To reach the island, take one of the regular ferries from Calasetta on Isola di Sant'Antioco just to the south, or from Portovesme on the Sardinian mainland, just south of Portoscuto. *Museo Civico: Fortino Carlo Emanuele III. Tel: 0781 855880. Open: summer Tue–Wed 5–9pm, Thur–Sat 9.30am–1pm & 5–9pm; winter Tue–Wed 5–9pm, Thur–Sat 9.30am–1pm & 3–7pm. Admission charge.*

Isola di Sant'Antioco

The larger of the two islands off the southwest corner of Sardinia, and the fourth-largest Italian island, Sant'Antioco is technically no longer an island and is reached by road from the mainland on a stone causeway first built by the Romans. You will see a section of their bridge on the right as you pass the coastline.

Aside from Sant'Antioco town itself, the **Museo Civico d'Arte Contemporanea di Calasetta** (Calasetta Civic Museum of Contemporary Art) has an excellent reputation for exhibitions and festivals. The permanent collection boasts over one hundred works. A regular ferry from Calasetta runs north to Carloforte on Isola di San Pietro (*see opposite*).

Around Calasetta there are some fine volcanic cliffs, with the best beach being at Spiaggia Le Saline. There are more and better beaches in

A view of the southern coast

the south of the island at Capo
Sperone on the very southern tip,
and the Spiaggia Canisoni, a long
stretch north of Maladroxia on the
sheltered eastern coast.
*Museo Civico d'Arte Contemporanea di
Calasetta: Via Savoia. Tel: 0781 840717.
Open: June–Aug Tue–Sun 6–9pm; rest of
the year Sat & Sun 5–8pm.*

Monte Sirai

The climb up Monte Sirai fills one
with a sense of expectation. The site
itself is impressive, with a long-range
view along the coast, though the
ancients would not have had to stare
at the unsightly refinery and mining
complexes that now sit in the
plains below.

Atop the hill is a wide plateau,
which has been settled since the
third millennium BC. When the
Phoenicians arrived in the 6th century
BC they built the first fortifications,
which were taken over by the
Carthaginians a century later. The town
site was abandoned in the 2nd century
BC. Archaeologists theorise that the
population was shipped off to a life
of slavery in Rome, and left for a
couple of thousand years until the
scientists moved in.

The street plan today remains just
as the last inhabitants saw it, with
long roads flanked by rows of neat
house walls that stand waist high.
It is easy to imagine a living
community with donkeys and carts
on the streets, and shops overflowing
with fruit and vegetables. A temple
to the Phoenician goddess Astarte
dominated the town square.

In a separate valley just north of the
town site, there is an ancient
necropolis, where the cremated remains
of Phoenicians were placed in special
carved chambers. A tophet (a sacred
place, where it is said that the
Carthaginians sacrificed children and
buried them as well as those who were
stillborn or died natural deaths) sits on
the hill above.
*4km (2¹/₂ miles) north of Carbonia. Tel:
0781 673966. Open: May–Oct Tue–Sun
9am–1pm & 3–8pm; Nov–Apr Tue–Sun
9am–5pm. Admission charge.*

Basilica of Sant'Antioco

Phoenician remains at Monte Sirai

Nora

In ancient times Nora was more important than Cágliari, but it somehow got left behind with the passage of time – in fact, left behind in the late Roman era.

Founded by the Phoenicians in one of the most sheltered bays on this part of the island, the city thrived on trade around the empire and was taken over with gusto by Punic forces and then by the Romans, who knew a good thing when they saw it.

The city occupied a wonderful site on a small peninsula, with the sea on two sides offering plenty of quayside capacity. Today, the rich remains offer an excellent picture of life in late Roman Sardinia and it does not take much imagination to picture the citizens about their daily lives. Archaeologists uncovered a plethora of excellent mosaic floors when they excavated the site. Many of these are still *in situ*, though they seem to have been relaid badly by the modern artisans and many of the tesserae are coming loose.

The **Casa dell'Atrio Tetrastilo** and the **Edificio Thermale** (public baths) have the finest and most complete examples, with a predominance of complicated geometric patterns that must have been a tiler's nightmare.

The Roman odeon in Nora

The theatre is rather small by Roman standards, an odeon rather than an amphitheatre. However, it benefited from the technological update of *dolii* – large terracotta vessels that were supposed to help with acoustics. The tallest walls still standing belong to the **Terme a Mare** (Sea Baths) on the coast of the western bay, where huge brick stacks sit at precarious angles, but it is the general quality of the whole that is impressive.

Finds from the site can be seen in the Archaeological Museum in Cágliari (*see p44*) and the Civic Museum in Pula (*see p65*).

3km (1³/4 miles) south of Pula. Open: 9am–sunset. Admission charge combined with Civic Museum in Pula.

Pula

The closest town to the remains at Nora, Pula is an expanding tourist destination, with a lively traditional centre. The Chiesa di Sant'Efisio was built in the 11th century on the site where the saint was said to have lost his head, having refused to renounce Christianity. Unfortunately it looks from the outside as if a modern two-storey house on the front of the earlier stone core has been added.

The **Museo Civico Patroni** (Patroni Civic Museum) is a repository for finds from Nora. There are many funerary artefacts, including ceramics, carved stele, a few personal items such as jewellery, plus a collection of sculptures representing various pagan gods.

Pro Loco (tourist office): Casa Frau, Piazza del Popolo. Tel: 346 3915381. Museo Civico Patroni: Corso Vittorio Emanuele 67. Tel: 070 9209610. Open: daily 9am–8pm. Admission charge combined with Nora Archaeological site.

Quartu Sant'Elena

Still a separate municipality, Quartu Sant'Elena is in the process of being swallowed by the suburbs of Cágliari. Its easy access to and from the capital means that it has grown rapidly in the last few years into the third-largest urban area on the island.

The name of the town, Quartu Sant'Elena, has a fascinating origin. It was originally called Quartu because it was founded on the site of a Roman milestone placed here *quartum miles* (i.e. 4 miles, or 6¹/₂ km) from Cágliari on the road north to Santa Teresa

A view of mountains near Pula

The south

Gallura. The name Sant'Elena, the patron saint of the town, was added as late as 1862.

The central area is compact with some good shopping, but you really should visit for the **Convento** (Capuchin Convent) built in 1631.

The town has a long tradition of bread-making because until recently it was surrounded by the maize fields of the Campidano plains. It is still well known for its festival breads and sweet pastries that are made by hand in numerous small family bakeries.

Sant'Antioco

This town, the largest on the island of Sant'Antioco, sits on the east coast facing the Sardinian mainland. The waterfront has a bustling atmosphere in summer, with numerous visiting yachts, but this is also a place where you can find fish being sold on the quayside, directly from small wooden boats.

The parish church of the same name at the top of the town has old antecedents, the present Romanesque edifice sitting on an earlier paleo-Christian basilica. This is where Saint Antioco is said to have found refuge when pursued by Roman forces in the early 2nd century. The interior is a melange of early architectural styles. The **Catacombe** (Catacombs) underneath the church are where Antioco has his home, in the chamber to the right of the altar. This is a fascinating series of carved chambers

A quiet corner in Sant'Antioco

started during the Punic era. They were usurped by the early Christian community as a burial ground. Some fragments of early frescoes show how ornate the catacombs would have been when in active use.

Just north of the town centre is a small and active **archaeological site** that has uncovered various sections of the Phoenician and Punic settlement that thrived here. Excavations have also revealed an important necropolis with evidence of over 3,000 cremations. The area is known to have been in uninterrupted use from 800 BC to the 1st century BC.

The major finds from the site are on display at the town's Archaeological Museum. The most dramatic is the collection of grave goods from the tophet, with stelae and urns containing the bones of animals and infants. Scientists are divided as to whether the babies died of natural causes or were sacrificed to the god Baal.

Museo Etnografico Su Magazinu 'e Su Binu (Su Magazinu 'e Su Binu Ethnographic Museum) explores the history of the traditional rural culture, with displays on cheese and wine-making and an interesting exhibit on byssus or 'sea-silk', produced in this region from the *Pinna nobilis* bivalve mollusc.

Tourist office: Piazza Repubblica 31. Tel: 0781 82031.

Catacombe: Open: Mon–Sat 9am–12.30pm & 3–8pm. Admission charge.
Museo Archeologico: Via Regina Margherita. Tel: 0781 841089; www.archeotur.it. Open: June–Sept Tue–Sun 9am–1pm & 3.30–7pm; Oct–May Tue–Sun 9am–1pm & 3.30–6pm. Admission charge.
Archaeological site: Tel: 0781 841089; www.archeotur.it. Open: daily June–Sept 9am–1pm & 3.30–7pm; Oct–Mar 9am–1pm & 3.30–6pm; closed Apr–May. Admission charge.
Museo Etnografico Su Magazinu 'e Su Binu: Via Necropoli 24. Tel: 0781 841089; www.archeotur.it.

A view of the waterfront at Sant'Antioco

*Open: June–Sept Tue–Sun 9am–1pm &
3.30–7pm; Oct–May Tue–Sun 9am–1pm
& 3.30–6pm. Admission charge.*

Sinnai

This small town, just north of Cágliari,
is famous throughout the island for its
Sardinian textiles. The cooperative in
town still produces excellent, though
expensive, examples.

Tempio d'Antas

The finest Roman temple site on
Sardinia, the Tempio d'Antas sits on
high ground with views across the
surrounding plains. In its heyday it
must have been splendid, but what
remains was re-erected by
archaeologists in the 1960s. The Ionic
columns support a pediment that
displays sections of Roman script
dedicated to Emperor Caracalla and the
god Sardus Pater Babai, a native
Sardinian Nuraghic deity, obviously a
typical attempt by Rome to integrate
native gods into the pantheon of
other gods worshipped throughout
the empire.
*15km (9¹/₂ miles) north of Iglesias. Open:
June–Sept daily 9am–1pm & 3–8pm;
Oct–May daily 9am–1pm & 3–6pm.
Admission charge.*

Villacidro

The art deco communal wash house
is a surprising find in the heart of this
small town, and is a fitting tribute to
its industrial heritage. The **Villa Leni
Museo Civico Archeologico** (Civic

Archaeology Museum) has an
interesting collection of Nuraghic finds
from the area, including a set of
stonecutting tools, copper ingots and
votive objects that include miniature
bronze *nuraghe.*

One kilometre (²/₃ mile) from the
town centre is the **Sa Spendula**
waterfall, a wonderful place to cool
after your tour.
*Villa Leni Museo Civico Archeologico:
Piazza Zampillo. Tel: 070 9310787.
Open: Mon–Fri 5–8pm, Sat–Sun
10am–1pm & 4–8pm. Admission charge.*

Villasimius

The largest town of the Costa Rei/Capo
Carbonara region, Villasimius used to
make a living out of charcoal and was
known as Carbonara until it petitioned
for a name change in 1862. The town
was only linked by road to Cágliari in
modern times, and the route between
the coast and the inland ranges of
Mount Arbu makes a very pretty trip
out of the capital.

The town **Museo Archeologico**
(Archaeological Museum) contains
rooms of artefacts discovered by marine
archaeologists in the waters offshore.
The bay was an important trading port
during the Byzantine era and finds
include cargos of amphorae and tiles.
A 15th-century Spanish galleon sunk off
Isola dei Cavoli has also been excavated
and produced a cache of weapons, seals
and beautiful ceramic *azulejos* (ornate
tiles produced in southern Spain and
Portugal). Another gallery displays finds

from **Is Coccureddus**, a Phoenician sanctuary overlooking the Gulf of Carbonara to the south of town that was important until the end of the Roman imperial cult in the 3rd century AD. The beaches to the southeast of the town are magnificent.

Tourist office: Piazza Giovanni XXIII Tel: 070 7928017.
Museo Archeologico: Via A Frau. Tel: 070 790023. Open: mid-June–mid-Sept Tue–Sun 10am–1pm & 9pm–midnight; mid-Sept–mid-June Fri–Sun 10am–1pm & 5–7pm. Admission charge.

The beach at Villasimius

Drive: The southwest

This drive mixes natural and historical attractions and offers plenty of opportunities for a little beach time.

Time: 6 hours.

Distance: 130km (81 miles).

Head out of the urban sprawl of Cágliari in the direction of Pula and you will soon pass the Stagno di Cágliari and Stagno di Santa Gilla on the right-hand side. Route 195 bypasses the industrial plants at Porto Foxi and after 30km (18¹/₂ miles) you will reach Pula.

1 Pula

The Museo Civico Patroni (Patroni Civic Museum) is a repository for finds from ancient Nora. The Chiesa di Sant'Efisio is located on the coast 3km (1³/₄ miles) south of Pula and was built in the 11th century on the site where the saint was beheaded by the Romans in the early 4th century.
From the church the ruins of Nora are just a few hundred metres to the west.

2 Nora

Nora was an important trading city until the end of the Roman era and the mosaics discovered here offer an excellent insight into how sophisticated life here must have been.

From Nora you will need to return to Pula before picking up the main 195 route, again travelling south signposted to Sant'Antioco. After 13km (8 miles) you will reach a junction to the left signposted Chia. Do not stay on the main road to Dómus de Maria. Once you have turned left, travel around 500m (¹/₃ mile), to the left turn to the beach at Chia.

3 Chia

This is a fantastic stretch of sand backed by areas of coastal marshland. It is a surfing and windsurfing beach, so you can spend some time watching the action on the waves.
Make your way back to the junction and turn left for the journey along the Costa del Sud.

4 Costa del Sud

This route leads around some majestic coastal bays and climbs to offer high-level views along the coast. There are numerous places to stop and get out of the car to take photos.

After 28km (17¹/₂ miles) the coast road meets up again with the 195. Turn right towards Teulada. Just as you enter the town look out for a left-hand turn to Santadi. Take this and after 14km (8¹/₂ miles) you will reach Grotte Is Zuddas.

5 Grotte Is Zuddas

The Zuddas caverns are huge with impressive stalactites and stalagmites plus rare crystal formations called helictites.

From the caverns continue on to Santadi, famous for its wedding festivals in early August. Once in town, take the route left for Villaperuccio and after 3km (1³/₄ miles) turn left at the crossroads in the direction of Giba. In the centre of Giba there will be a turning right to Tratalias, past the shores of Lago di Monte Pranu. At the new town of Tratalias, turn left and Chiesa di Santa Maria will appear after 1km (²/₃ mile).

6 Chiesa di Santa Maria

Founded in 1213 in the old town of Tratalias, this rather austere Romanesque church was the cathedral of the surrounding diocese until the seat was moved to Iglesias (*see pp59–60*) in 1503.

Leave the church in a westerly direction towards Sant'Antioco. The road crosses the 195 by bridge and then feeds into the 126 for the journey across to the island. The narrow isthmus carrying the modern road is not the same as that started by the Phoenicians and finished by the Romans but leads you to the same place, Sant'Antioco.

7 Sant'Antioco

Explore the ancient remains and the catacombs of the Chiesa di Sant'Antioco before heading down to the waterfront for a well-deserved espresso.

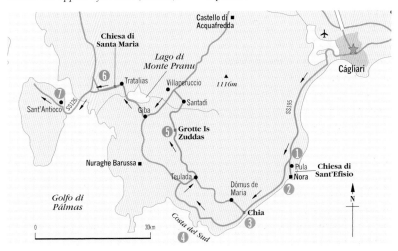

Cork

The cork harvest has been one of the chief export products from Sardinia for hundreds of years. It is an important natural industry and one of the few non-timber forest product industries in the world. Harvested from the hardy cork oak (*Quercus suber*), cork is a renewable resource and the process produces no wastage from the crop. The most important product is natural bottle stoppers (usually for wine), so much so that we also call them 'corks'. They account for 70 per cent of cork revenues. Flooring, soundproofing material and decorative items make up the bulk of the rest.

Why cork?

Cork is one of nature's gifts to us. It has a lightweight, flexible honeycomb structure and is impermeable to liquids and gases. It is fire and rot resistant, soft and buoyant.

Where?

Cork oaks are found throughout the southwestern Mediterranean. In addition to Sardinia, the main producers are mainland Italy, Spain and Portugal, though the coastline of North Africa also contributes.

Currently there are over 2,000,000 hectares (5,000,000 acres) under cork oak in Europe and the industry is estimated to employ 30,000 people.

Harvesting

Harvesting does not kill the tree and if harvested correctly each oak can live to an age of 200 years.

New trees are not harvested until they reach the age of 25; then they must be left for between nine and 12 years before they can be stripped again (on Sardinia, harvesting is regulated at every 12 years). The first harvest is not suitable to be used for wine corks, and the tree must be 40 years old before the first wine cork quality crop. After cutting, the trees

Products covered in cork

A pile of cork left to dry

are marked with a number and the date noted for the records.

Cork is harvested in spring or summer as the tree is in growth cycle. Regrowth being quickest at this time, it is safer for the tree. Harvesting is a highly skilled job when specially designed cutting tools are used. An experienced harvester can cut 600kg (1,320lb) per day.

How cork stoppers are made

The newly harvested cork is cut into thick short sheets. It is washed and graded and the round stoppers are punched directly from it. These are then graded, sterilised and their moisture content checked. Finally they are hygienically sealed into polythene bags and shipped. Seventeen million are punched every year. Any residue from this process is ground up and compacted to produce cork tiles or thin cork sheets.

The future

The development of synthetic corks has been hailed as an environmental breakthrough, but nothing could be further from the truth. Synthetic corks take longer to degrade than natural corks and the increased market share of synthetic corks threatens cork production and a whole associated ecosystem.

The World Wildlife Fund has come out in defence of the industry, saying it is 100 per cent environmentally friendly. Harvesting cork causes no damage to the forest and in fact the industry supports a whole range of wildlife. A drop in demand might result in cork oaks being ripped up and a more profitable and less environmentally friendly crop being put in its place. The long lead time needed before first harvest means that, once gone, the forests will be almost impossible to replace.

The west

Bounded by the wilds of the Barbagia and Gennargentu to the east, Monte Ferru to the north and Monte Linas to the south, the west comprises the vast Campidano plain. In addition to being a fertile agricultural region it also boasts Sardinia's largest coastal marshes and salt flats, plus a wealth of historical remains from fine Nuraghic villages to Roman cities to early Christian churches.

The history of the region is littered with bouts of malaria and spoiled harvests, problems that have only been solved in the last century with the arrival of modern insecticides and the draining of hundreds of thousands of hectares for farmland. Today, it is one of the most popular birdwatching areas in Europe and has some sublime beaches scattered along the coast.

Arborea

Though the name sounds old, Arborea was founded during the 1930s and was one of Mussolini's pet projects on land reclaimed from the coastal marshes. The communal piazza still has the feel of regimented order with its topiary and flower beds, and the municipal buildings have a sort of utilitarian art deco look that will attract lovers of modern architecture. Otherwise, the **Collezione Civica Archeologica** (Municipal Archaeological Collection), with a small collection of ancient finds, mostly domestic relics, will be the highlight.

Mussolini's dream was to make Italy self-sufficient in as many raw materials as possible, and this is one of the reasons why the almost spent mines just south of here were reopened. The drained marshlands were to provide Sardinia and the mainland with food, and even today it supplies copious amounts of rice, cereals, fruit such as watermelon and strawberries, plus a vast range of vegetables.
Collezione Civica Archeologica: Viale Omodeo 5. Tel: 0783 80331.
Open: Mon–Fri 10am–1pm.
Admission free.

Arbus

Home to one of Sardinia's well-known traditional knives and its most famous modern exponent, Paolo Pusceddu, who not only produces beautiful handmade tools but has also founded a museum to the craft on the site of his workshop.

The **Museo del Coltello** (Knife Museum) follows the use of blades

Western Sardinia

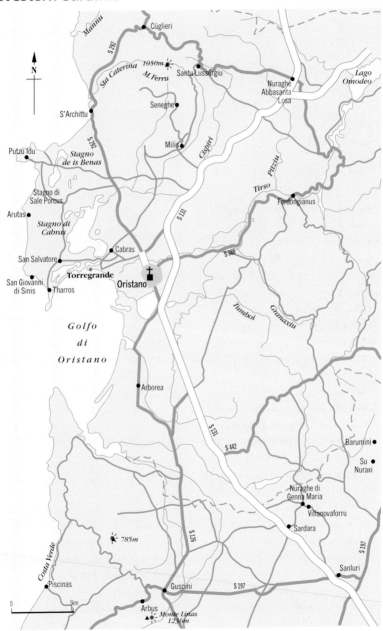

Tharros finds in Cabras Museum

from Neolithic flint and obsidian tools used for skinning animals and slicing raw meat, to the first metal blades, to fine fighting swords and obviously fine examples of the different Sardinian knives. Paolo also is holder of the official world record for the 'largest pocket knife in the world' weighing a massive 80kg (176lb) and measuring 3.65m (12ft) in length – that is some pocket! There is a video on the process of making an Arbus knife, and you can buy from the shop on site knowing that you have a unique souvenir and that you are supporting a rare and important traditional craft.

Museo del Coltello: Via Roma 15. Tel: 070 9759220; www.museodelcoltello.it. Open: 9am–12.30pm & 3.30–7pm. Admission free.

Cabras

Museo Civico G Marongiu is a rather ugly modern building, but the galleries have a wealth of finds from Tharros (*see pp85–7*) and ancient sites in the surrounding countryside.

There is an interesting exhibit about the 'Su Fassoni' traditional reed boats that were used by fishermen on the salt flats for hundreds of years until the 1970s. Similar to those used in ancient Egypt, they were made by hand and lasted about three months before the fibre broke down, allowing water to soak into the structure, whereupon the fishermen had to make a new one. A shame these eco-friendly craft are not still being made!

The other artefacts are arranged in rooms in chronological order showing the development of many skills from building to metalworking to pottery production. Shards of pottery and naive pieces from the Il Sinis Neolithic site (5th–4th century BC) contrast with beautiful jewellery from the Necropolis of Arrius, which dates from the same time. The Tharros finds show the richness of life in this ancient town, with numerous oil lamps, glass vessels, ceramics and small carved domestic and religious statues. There is monument decoration too, like the weathered grave stele found at the tophet alongside the terracotta urns that held cremated human remains.

Back in the town, the **Chiesa di Maggiore** (Santa Maria Assunta) plays a significant role in one of the region's most important festivals, the Barefoot Race (*see p83*). (*See also* Stagno di Cabras, *p85*.)

Museo Civico G Marongiu: Via Tharros. Tel: 0783 290636. Open: summer daily 9am–1pm & 4–8pm; winter Tue–Sun 9am–1pm & 3–7pm. Admission charge (combined with Tharros ancient site).

Fordongianus

The hot mineral springs at Fordongianus, in the foothills of the Barbagia, were where the Romans came for a little R&R after business at Tharros. The remains of the **Terme Romane** (Roman Spa) indicate that this must have been a wonderful place for a sauna and massage in the early centuries of the

first millennium, with fine fountains and ornate communal pools. One pool set below a fine arcade still holds water.

The other attraction in town is the **Casa Aragonese** (Aragonese House) erected during the 16th century. Renovated in the 1980s, it is a fine example of unadulterated Catalan-Gothic domestic architecture, with beautifully carved details on stone door and window lintels.

Terme Romane: Tel: 0783 60157. Open: summer Tue–Sun 9.30am–1pm & 3–7.30pm; winter Tue–Sun 9am–1pm & 3–6pm. Admission charge. Casa Aragonese: Open: summer Tue–Sun 9am–1pm & 3–7pm; winter Tue–Sun 9am–1pm & 2.30–5pm. Admission charge.

The Chiesa di Maggiore in Cabras

Ruins of a *nuraghe*

Guspini

The ores of the Montevecchio have been exploited since Nuraghic times, giving a rich seam of lead and zinc until the modern age. Today, the 19th-century mine workings and their neo-Gothic pithead buildings have been renovated to create the island's premier mining museum, **La Civiltà Mineraria**. The **Palazzo della Direzione** (Director's Mansion) shows just what a lordly life the owners had on the back of the effort made by the workers. The house has been expertly finished with a wealth of gold leaf and ornate architrave. The mansion has some interesting late 19th- and 20th-century photos, documents and other official bits and pieces.

Back in town, the **Chiesa di Santa Maria di Malta** was founded during the Byzantine era but renovated and enlarged circa 1200. The façade is an interesting amalgam of carved stone and lime-washed stucco. It was at one time under the auspices of the Knights Hospitallers of Malta.

On the outskirts of town is a natural basalt cliff that is one of the finest of its kind in the Mediterranean.

La Civiltà Mineraria: Montevecchio. Tel: 070 97601. Open: Sat & Sun 9am–1pm & 2.20–5.20pm, on other days by appointment. Admission charge.

Monte Ferru

This verdant volcanic cone breaks the Campidano plain to the north of Oristano and is worth a tour by car to enjoy the contrast both in temperature and in lifestyle. A series of villages are scattered along the route around the foothills, the largest of which is **Santu Lussúrgiu** (*see p84*).

On the northern flank of the mountain, Cuglieri is crowned by the remains of Castello Monte Ferru, built in the wake of the Vandal invasion. The fort formed the frontier between the Arborea and Alghero Giudicati during medieval times. **Museo dell'Olio** (Museum of the Olive) gives an insight into olive oil production in the area, and the 17th-century **Cattedrale di Santa Maria della Neve** is one of the largest churches on the island, though size is not everything and the interior is a disappointment.

To the south, Seneghe is another village famed for its fine olive oil, and closer to Oristano, on the south side of Monte Ferru, is Milis, where you will find **Museo del Gioiello e del Costume Sardo** (Museum of Sardinian Jewellery and Costume), a small but high-quality collection of jewellery and

traditional costumes that are still worn with great pride during the island's numerous festivals. Sadly, the museum is only open during the build-up to these festivals.

Check with the tourist office in Oristano for opening times. Museo dell'Olio: Corso Umberto 68. Tel: 0785 39820. Open: Tue–Sun 10am–1pm & 4–8pm. Admission charge. Museo del Gioiello e del Costume Sardo: Palazzo Boyl, Piazza Martiri, Milis. Tel: 0783 51665. Open only during festivals. Admission free.

Nuraghe Abbasanta Losa

More like a mini medieval castle than an ancient building, Abbasanta Losa is one of the more impressive Nuraghe complexes. An unusual triangular main tower, surrounded by three smaller round structures, it dates from *c.* 1500 BC. There is a narrow central corridor leading to small rooms and sets of stairs. It is easy to get an appreciation of the building quality from the interior views.

5km (3 miles) west of Abbasanta. Open: daily 9am–1pm & 3–7pm. Admission charge.

Nuraghe di Genna Maria

Genna Maria started out as a conical tower but was later expanded into a triangular structure similar to that at Abbasanta Losa. Surrounding this was a series of stone houses and an outer defensive wall. The settlement expanded throughout the Bronze Age but was empty by the time the

The Duomo in Oristano

ancient votive items and pottery, there are finer Carthaginian and Roman artefacts, including coins, glass jars and jewellery.

7km (4¹/4 miles) northeast of Sardara. Open: daily 9am–1pm & 3.30–7pm. Admission charge.
Museo Archeologico: Piazza Constituzione 1, Villanovaforru. Tel: 070 915548. Open: Tue–Sun 9.30am–1pm & 3.30–7pm. Admission charge.

Oristano

Set at the heart of the vast Campidano plain, Oristano is a small, busy city with a warm atmosphere and certainly deserves a few hours' attention. The tourist office is well equipped with information about the surrounding countryside.

Oristano was the capital of Arborea province during the Giudicati era and the home town of one of Sardinia's fondest-remembered heroines, Eleonora, who fought the Catalan forces but failed in her attempt to keep the region independent. Her statue graces one of the main squares in town, where you will also find the tourist office, the Municipio (Town Hall), once the 19th-century Palazzo Campus Colona, and a feast of gently faded neoclassical façades.

That the Spanish took full control of the town is seen in the architecture: in the fine wrought-iron balconies of the grand mansions on Corso Umberto I and the simple whitewashed walls of humbler abodes on the streets around.

Carthaginians arrived. They usurped the site as a pagan temple.

In the village of Villanovaforru nearby there is a **Museo Archeologico** (Archaeological Museum) with finds from Genna Maria and the many other Nuraghic settlements and sites scattered across the Marmilla region, as this area of Sardinia is known. In addition to

ORISTANO'S HORSE RACE

The last Sunday and last Tuesday of Carnival see one of Sardinia's most colourful spectacles, the Sartiglia, two tournaments surrounded by a riot of medieval pageantry, where the riders must collect wooden rings on the end of their jousting poles. The whole event is filled with ceremonial pomp and age-old ritual watched by crowds of thousands.

THE CAVIAR OF ORISTANO

Bottarga is a speciality of the Oristano region. Pressed mullet roe that is dried and comes in the shape of a sausage, it is served sliced as an antipasto or eaten with spaghetti and warm olive oil.

The main town museum is the **Antiquarium Arborense** (Ancient Arborea), housed in the 17th-century Palazzo Parpaglia, a treasure trove of finds from ancient sites that dot the plains, including many from Tharros (*see pp85–7*). Artefacts include funerary and votive offerings but also a large carved statue thought to be of the god Baal, an eastern deity brought west by the Phoenicians. The medieval era is also well represented with carved coats of arms, paintings and documents. Make sure you visit the *pinacoteca* or Art Gallery on site, where you will be able to view the *Retablo di Sant Christ*, a fine painting by Pietro Cavero, one of the masters of Sardinian art.

Oristano once sat within proud city walls, but there are only a couple of fragments remaining. These include the Torre di Mariano II, a fine upstanding watchtower that once marked an entryway into the enclave and offers panoramic views from its upper level (not open regular hours), and the more diminutive Portixedda or 'little gate'.

The town's main place of worship is the **Duomo**, a Gothic skeleton on which hangs a baroque ensemble. Eleonora is said to be buried in **Chiesa di Santa Chiara** on the other side of

the old town. The façade of Chiesa di San Francesco has a splendid neoclassical portico, but the dramatic polychrome *crocefisso* (wooden sculpture of the Crucifixion) by Nicodemo in the interior dates from the 14th century.

The municipality of Oristano has invested in a communal cycle rental project, and at several points around the town, including Piazza Eleonora,

Statue of Eleonora in Oristano

A warm sunny day at S'Archittu bay

you can pick up a bike between 7am and 9pm to tour the city.

Tourist office: Piazza Eleonora.
Tel: 0783 36831.
Antiquarium Arborense: Piazzetta
Corrias. Tel: 0783 791262. Open:
Tue–Sun 9am–2pm & 3–8pm.
Admission charge.
Duomo: Piazza del Duomo. Open: daily
9am–noon & 4–8pm.
Chiesa di Santa Chiara: Via Santa
Chiara. Open: daily 9am–noon &
3.30–7.30pm.

Putzu Idu

The surfers of Oristano head out to Putzu Idu, a point on the coast to the north of town. The limestone cliffs around the point make a dramatic contrast to the flat marshlands only a dozen or so kilometres (7 to 8 miles) to the south. Inland from the beach is the **Stagno di Sale Porcus**, an unspoiled brackish lake and marshland that is being studied by scientists from the World Wildlife Fund.

South of the point are the vast sands of Arutas, a pure white with the consistency of tiny marbles worn smooth by the action of the sea. It is like walking on a sugary carpet.

S'Archittu

The coastline around S'Archittu contrasts greatly with the flat bays around Oristano. The limestone cliffs have been cut and carved into numerous little bays and rocky bluffs, and several small resorts dot the coast. Inland are the sites of ancient Cornus, a *nuraghe* necropolis, while the Torre del Pozzo scans the seas offshore.

San Giovanni di Sinis

Set among the wild beauty of the far-reaching salt flats, the tiny village of San Giovanni di Sinis makes a great starting point for birdwatching trips. It is also the closest spot to Tharros for refreshments and a snack. The **Basilica di San Giovanni di Sinis** is what lends its name to the surrounding settlement. An archetypal Byzantine structure, it is a fascinating example of late 5th- and early 6th-century religious architecture and is dedicated to John the Baptist.

THE BAREFOOT RACE

In 1506 the Moors attacked the village of San Salvatore and the villagers had to flee in the middle of the night. The morning after, a few men returned barefoot to save the remains of the saint, which were left behind in the church in the panic of the night before. Luckily the bones had not been desecrated and they were transported post-haste to the parish church in neighbouring Cabras. This journey was commemorated every year with a barefoot procession and it only became a race in the 20th century when the young men began to include an element of competition in the proceedings.

Today the race is part of nine days of ceremonies. On the first Saturday in September youths take the statue of the saint from the sanctuary at Chiesa di Maggiore (Santa Maria Assunta) in Cabras and run with it the 8km (5 miles) to San Salvatore. On the following Sunday they make the journey in reverse.

Later additions brought the footprint to the Latin cross shape in the 11th century, but the church fell into disuse in the second millennium and was used as a sheep-pen for many decades. Repairs began in 1836 and the church was restored again in 1965 and 1994. Note the ornate stone font on the right as you enter the church. This is a fine baroque piece that dates from the 16th century.

San Salvatore

You may recognise the streets of simple whitewashed cottages in San Salvatore as soon as you arrive. During the 1960s many scenes from spaghetti westerns were filmed here, and, despite the gentrification of one or two, the overall impression is that nothing much has changed since then and the place has the feel of an empty film set; you could imagine a fast-drawing, cheroot-smoking bandit stepping out of the shadows at any moment.

At the heart of the tiny settlement is the **Chiesa di San Salvatore**, a simple Romanesque structure built to house the remains of the saint – though they are now under the auspices of Chiesa di Maggiore (Santa Maria Assunta) in Cabras (*see pp76–7*). The Romanesque church sits on the site of a pagan Roman temple dated 3rd century AD, which you reach down a narrow flight of stairs in the centre of the floor. The subterranean sanctuary has several chambers with an altar room at the far end. Aside from the nine

The Basilica di San Giovanni di Sinis

days during the festival in early September, the church is only open to pre-booked tours.

Santu Lussúrgiu

The houses of the old town tumble down the sheer flanks of the ancient volcanic crater of Monte Ferru (*see p79*). It is a lovely place to get lost among the maze of narrow cobbled streets, though there are no real attractions aside from the tiny **Museo della Tecnologia Contadina** (Museum of Rural Technology), which displays all the local traditional industries, from weaving to bread-making. There is also an old still for making *filu e ferru*. There are excellent views across the rooftops from the site of the huge statue of Christ that stands on an outcrop to the northwest of the town.

Museo della Tecnologia Contadina: Via D Meloni, Santu Lussúrgiu. Tel: 0783 550617. Open: summer daily 10am–noon & 6–8pm; winter daily 10am–noon & 4–6pm. Admission charge.

Sardara

Surrounded by mineral springs, the site of this small town was a popular place for Phoenicians to celebrate their water deities in the 6th and 5th centuries BC. Today, modern Italians come to take the waters for the putative medicinal benefits.

Visit the **Museo Civico Archeologico Villa Abbas** (Villa Abbas Municipal Archaeological Museum) while you are here. Several excavated Nuraghic graves unearthed at Terr'e Cresia nearby have been recreated in every detail and it is fascinating to see the grave goods lying with the bones of these sophisticated ancient peoples. A pair of 8th-century BC bronze archers is an undoubted highlight of the small but worthwhile collection.

The beautiful parish church, **Chiesa di San Gregorio**, is interesting because the building spans the Romanesque and Gothic styles; the church is taller than is generally accepted in classic Romanesque, with carved decoration that falls between the rounded Romanesque arch and the pointed Gothic.

Museo Civico Archeologico Villa Abbas: Piazza Liberta. Tel: 070 9386183. Open: Tue–Sun 9am–1pm & 5–8pm. Admission charge.

Stagno di Cabras (Cabras Lake)

One of the largest lagoons in Europe, the Stagno di Cabras is a prime birdwatching site and a wonderful wide-open area in which to walk and cycle. Wetlands all across Europe are under threat from land reclamation and urban expansion, but this region is now protected.

Details about the species can be found on an information plaque just outside Cabras village on the road to San Salvatore (in English and Italian).

From here, even if there is no bird life on view, there are wonderful views across the water to the pastel-hued buildings of Cabras and a foot/cycle/bridal path that leads around the lake: the full network totals over 40km (25 miles), and it is not realistic to attempt to tackle it all.

During the summer you can find boatmen offering trips to explore the reed beds and other ecosystems around the lake. It makes a nice trip even if you are not interested in the wildlife.

Su Nuraxi

Considered by scientists to be the finest example of ancient Nuraghic architecture, UNESCO added Su Nuraxi to its list of World Heritage Sites in the late 1990s. The site has a large *nuraghe* surrounded by a triangular battlement with four intact towers, and is an excellent example of the type, though only the base level of the three-storey building is still extant.

Surrounding the *nuraghe* is the largest ancient village site on Sardinia with the remains of over 50 houses and other structures with their circular walls looking rather like the inside of a conch shell if you cut it in half. Archaeologists have been able to identify one as a miller's house and another as a stonemason's house.

Barumini (60km/37 miles southeast of Oristano). Open: summer daily 9am–8pm; winter daily 9am–6pm. Admission charge.

Tharros

Set on the tip of a narrow peninsula in the north of the Gulf of Oristano and sheltered from the prevailing winds, Tharros was an important city throughout the late Bronze Age and the Classical era. The remains today give

The Nuraghe at Su Nuraxi

hints of the urbane lifestyle of the inhabitants. Much of the town was built of dark and dense volcanic rock that is particularly hard-wearing. The most important architectural feature is the drainage system that runs along all the main streets. This did an excellent job of carrying sewage and dirty water out of the city, keeping the air relatively fresh. These streets are well preserved with slabs of stone walked on by Roman sandals and marked by ancient cart tracks. The main route, Cardo Maximus, is the finest of these. Rising up through the residential area from the waterfront, it leads to the site of the temple of Demeter and the tophet.

The city was founded by the Phoenicians in the 8th century BC and became a major naval stronghold and trading port when the Carthaginians took the island. Under the Romans it continued to thrive and became an episcopal seat in the early years of Christianity. The site was populated until the 11th century but was abandoned during the pirate raids that plagued the coast in this era. However, the city certainly has seen changes since then. The massive port structure that was the economic heartbeat of the city now lies under the water, plus a huge amount of stone was shipped off to the new settlement of Oristano just around the bay.

The myriad walls already excavated belonged mostly to domestic and commercial buildings interesting only for their sheer number. A small Roman thermal complex now close to the water's edge was converted into a paleo-Christian church in the 3rd century AD and expanded into a full basilica towards the end of the first millennium. A larger baths complex sits further west, and constitutes the most complete remains on the site.

Above the archaeological attraction but set on the area of the ancient acropolis sits the **Torre di San Giovanni**, built with stone recycled from the city. At 14.5m (14ft 9in) in diameter, it is one of the largest of Sardinia's many coastal towers and was manned until 1846.

15km (9¹/₂ miles) west of Oristano.
Tel: 0783 370019.
Open 9am–sunset.
Admission charge combined with the Archaeological Museum in Cabras (see pp76–7).

The west

The ruins of Tharros are an important archaeological site

Drive: Oristano and around

The flat plains around Oristano offer an excellent and easy drive linking some of its most important historical attractions without having to travel very far.

Time: 4 hours.

Distance: 50km (31 miles).

1 Oristano

Oristano has several attractions and is particularly enjoyable during the morning when people are about their daily business. Visit the Antiquarium Arborense for its ancient finds, and the Duomo. Stroll along Corso Umberto I with its range of shops to Torre di Mariano II or enjoy a bike ride. The commune provides bikes for use within the municipal boundaries.

Leave Oristano, travelling north, following signs for Cabras. Soon after you cross the river 2km (1¹/₄ miles) outside the town centre, turn left to Cabras.

2 Cabras town centre

The town centre is graced by the Chiesa di Maggiore (Santa Maria Assunta) and on the main road south of town is the Museo Civico, with finds from Tharros and other surrounding ancient sites, plus some interesting insights into the traditional industries on the salt basins that surround the town. Cabras sits on the banks of the Stagno di Cabras, which, along with neighbouring smaller lakes, offers an exceptional natural environment for flora and fauna.

From the museum turn right and go straight across at the next junction to Torregrande.

3 Torregrande

The Golfo di Oristano's beach resort has an excellent and sheltered stretch of sand. Perfect for a family pit stop.

Retrace your route to the Cabras junction and turn left in the direction of Tharros. Just after the junction you will see the southern shores of the Stagno di Cabras on the right with an information area. After 7km (4¼ miles) the road leads to San Salvatore. Turn right into the village and parking area.

4 San Salvatore

A film set for spaghetti westerns throughout the 1960s, the simple single-storey cottages of San Salvatore have changed little since then. In the heart of town, the tiny early Romanesque Chiesa di San Salvatore incorporates a subterranean 3rd-century AD Roman temple, but it is rarely open except during the festivals of early September.

From San Salvatore, continue towards Tharros. Just before you reach the archaeological park after 4.5km (2¾ miles) turn right at the village of San Giovanni di Sinis.

The beach at Torregrande

5 San Giovanni di Sinis

The tiny Basilica of San Giovanni di Sinis is one of the most complete early Christian churches on the island. The whole edifice was completed by the 11th century, but the basic square at its heart is a 5th- or early 6th-century place of worship, built just after the Vandal attacks and with very clear Byzantine architectural details: no columns and a semi-circular apse.

You can walk from the village to Tharros site (about 500m/⅓ mile): indeed in summer it may not be possible to find parking closer to the site as the car parks get full with beachgoers; or take the car and park outside the ticket office.

6 Tharros

Tharros is an impressive site in scale and layout, though the remains of the monumental buildings are disappointing due to much of the stone being recycled for use at Oristano. Enjoy walking the well-paved roads with their communal drainage channels.

Return along the main road on which you travel back to San Salvatore and on to the main Oristano–Bosa road. Turn right here for the 2.5km (1½-mile) journey back into Oristano.

Drive: Around Monte Ferru

Take a drive north of Oristano and you can combine visits to historical sites with an hour or two on the beach and some spectacular views of the countryside. It is a wonderfully varied journey.

Time: 6 hours.

Distance: 110km (68 miles).

1 Oristano

Start the day at Oristano. It would be a great idea to take breakfast here, in one of the cafés on Corso Umberto I or Piazza Roma, where you can enjoy views from Torre di Mariano II. Visit the Duomo and the Antiquarium Arborense. *Leave Oristano travelling north following signs for Cabras. Soon after you cross the river outside town turn left to Cabras.*

2 Cabras

The main attraction in Cabras is the Museo Civico. It holds some fine finds from Tharros and other surrounding ancient sites, plus some interesting insights into the traditional lifestyles in the salt basins that surround the town. *From the museum turn right, and right again at the next junction in the direction of Tharros. Just after the junction you will see the southern shores of the Stagno di Cabras on the right with an information area with pictures of common and migratory species. You*

may spot flamingoes here. After 7km (4¼ miles) the road leads to San Salvatore. Turn right into the village and parking area.

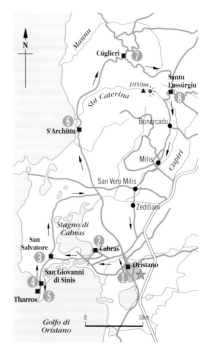

3 San Salvatore

A film set for spaghetti westerns throughout the 1960s, the simple single-storey cottages of San Salvatore have changed little since then. In the heart of town, the tiny early Romanesque Chiesa di San Salvatore incorporates a subterranean 3rd-century AD Roman temple.

Continue towards Tharros. Just before you reach the archaeological park after 4.5km (2³/₄ miles) turn right at the village of San Giovanni di Sinis.

San Salvatore

4 San Giovanni di Sinis

The tiny Basilica of San Giovanni di Sinis is one of the most complete early Christian churches on the island.

You can walk from the village to Tharros site (about 500m/¹/₃ mile) or take the car.

5 Tharros

Tharros is an impressive site in scale and layout, though the remains of the monumental buildings are disappointing due to much of the stone being recycled for use at Oristano.

Return along the main road on which you travel back to San Salvatore. Turn left here, signposted Riola Sardo and Putzu Idu. Carry on until the road meets a T-junction with the Oristano–Bosa road (16km/10 miles). Turn left here towards Bosa and Cúglieri. Travel on for 13km (8 miles) to reach S'Archittu.

6 S'Archittu

The coastline here comprises small sandy coves and eroded bluffs and outcrops. There are also a few restaurants and cafés for refreshment.

From S'Archittu continue north until you reach Cúglieri (15km/9¹/₂ miles).

7 Cúglieri

Cúglieri has vestiges of a medieval castle and a large cathedral. The Olive Oil Museum depicts one of the island's major export industries.

From Cúglieri, turn east on the road that leads into the hills in the direction of Santu Lussúrgiu 18km (11 miles) away.

8 Santu Lussúrgiu

Santu Lussúrgiu is a maze of cobbled streets that clings to the edge of an ancient volcanic crater, which is an atmospheric place to explore.

From Santu Lussúrgiu follow the road south to Oristano, travelling through the villages of Bonárcado, Milis, San Vero Milis and Zeddiani before reaching Oristano itself.

Drive: Around Monte Ferru

The northwest

The northwest is Sardinia's most varied region. To be sure, you can find superb beaches, the raw material of any island getaway, but there's so much to see inland that you won't mind missing a morning or two of sunbathing. This area plays host to several of the island's most visually pleasing towns, from the fortified Spanish-style citadel of Alghero to the Italianate mansions of Sassari – and some of its most enjoyable shopping, too.

Out in the countryside you will find more than a few ancient sites. The number of *nuraghi* vying for your attention are only surpassed by the bell towers of medieval Pisan churches that gaze out over hill and vale.

Alghero

Founded by the Catalans when they first took control of the island, Alghero remains a Spanish town on Italian soil. Some of the old folk still speak an ancient Catalan dialect and within the walls of the old citadel there's a definite Iberian feel to the streets. Today it is Sardinia's most alluring tourist town, with a busy harbour full of bobbing tour boats and a wealth of shopping and eating opportunities, plus gorgeous sandy beaches just a couple of kilometres north along the bay.

Three curtains of the original city wall are pretty much intact, making the narrow maze of alleyways and streets easy to explore. Aside from the fortifications themselves, Piazza Civica

is perhaps the architectural highlight, a cobbled square lined with medieval palazzos, the finest being Palazzo Albis, from where Charles V addressed the populace in 1541.

The neoclassical façade of **Cattedrale di Santa Maria** (Duomo) seems overlarge for its piazza, but the interior is an enjoyable mix of Catalan-Gothic and Renaissance elements, with baroque trimmings. Next door, the **Museo Diocesano** (Diocese Museum) displays many of the cathedral's treasures, including a holy relic: a reliquary containing bones from one of the *innocenti* (babes killed by Herod in the days after Jesus was born).

Two other churches worthy of note in the old town are the **Chiesa di San Michele** on Via Carlo Alberto, with its multi-hued majolica-tiled roof and baroque interior, and the **Chiesa di San Francesco,** also on Via Carlo Alberto, which was rebuilt after a partial collapse of the older edifice in 1593. Sections of the Romanesque church can still be seen: the façade is a fascinating amalgam of Romanesque and a late Renaissance addition.

The landward walls of the castle were demolished as the town grew in the 18th century and a series of squares and gardens roughly follow their ground plan, neatly dividing the old town from the new. Two towers remain: the D-shaped **Torre di Porto Terra,** which protected one of the two entrances and guarded a drawbridge at one time, and **Torre di San Giovanni,**

which now houses the **Museo Virtuale** (*Largo S Francesco. Tel: 079 9734045. Open: June & Sept 11am–1pm & 6–9pm, July & Aug 11am–1pm & 7–10pm, Oct–Mar 10am–1pm, closed Apr–May. Admission charge*).

There are few attractions in the new part of town, but it does play host to Sardinia's only aquarium, **Mare Nostrum Aquarium**, a small but varied collection of sea creatures and reptiles. However, kids may have more fun spotting wild fish swimming on one of

The northwest

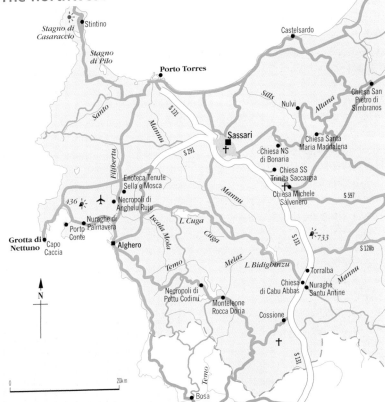

The city wall of Alghero

the many boat tours, the most popular being to the Grotto of Neptune (*see p96*) out across the bay.

Cattedrale bell tower: Open: July–Sept Tue, Thur, Sat 7–9.30pm. Admission charge. Oct–June, guided tour by request. Admission charge.

Museo Diocesano: Piazza Duomo. Tel: 079 9733041. Open: July–Aug 10am–12.30pm & 7–11pm; June & Sept 10am–noon & 6–9pm; Mar–May 10am–12.30pm & 5–8pm; Oct–Dec 10am–12.30pm; Jan–Feb by appointment. Admission charge.

Mare Nostrum Aquarium: Via XX Settembre 1. Tel: 079 978333. Open: Aug daily 10am–1.30pm, 5pm–12.30am; July & Sept 10am–1pm & 5–11pm; June & Oct 10am–1pm & 4–9pm; May 10am–1pm & 3–7pm; Nov–Apr Sat, Sun & holidays 3–8pm. Admission charge.

Bosa

Set on the banks of the Temo River, Bosa makes a wonderful impression as you approach from the northwest. A striking multicoloured town set below an impressive medieval castle, it is further enhanced by its riverside setting.

The town sits on the north bank of the river, which is the only navigable watercourse on the island. To the south, there is a neglected but historic district of old tanneries, that are crying out to be transformed into a pretty waterside hotel or shopping/restaurant complex with alfresco dining and views across to the fishing boats tied up against the bank. The town was founded in Roman times, but the Malaspina family breathed new life into it when they arrived and built the castle in the 12th century. Bosa went into gentle decline

A SPINY SPECIALITY

Alghero shows its Catalan roots by being the main town serving speciality seafood. Spiny lobster and sea urchin are both popular – though the prices (on menus the price listed is per kilogram) can be on the steep side.

with the coming of the modern world, and the streets have a wonderful time-worn quality. Nestled into small piazzas are churches such as the baroque **Chiesa del Carmine.** The town's main place of worship is the rococo (or Piedmontese baroque, as it is known on Sardinia) **Cattedrale dell'Immacolata**, set on a small square punctuating the long main street, Corso Vittorio Emanuele, which is flanked by fine three- and four-storey mansions with cafés, restaurants and shops. Behind the cathedral you have access to the stone bridge over the river. There is also a footbridge that crosses over to the far end of the tanneries.

The major town museum is housed in **Casa Deriu**, a mansion erected in the 1800s. The first floor is furnished in typical style, while the second floor offers historical background to the now defunct tanning industry that had its heyday in the 19th century.

The castle is in the grips of a comprehensive renovation programme but is the finest remaining fortification of its kind on Sardinia. The church inside the compound has a renowned fresco cycle and there are magnificent views from the walls.

The former **Cattedrale di San Pietro Extramuros** (so named because it sits outside the confines of the town) is 1,500m (1 mile) upstream along the south bank of the river and is a mostly Romanesque body with a younger, Gothic face.

Two kilometres (1¼ miles) from the town is the modern Bosa marina resort

A view of Bosa quayside and town

One of Bosa's old narrow streets

with a good-sized beach and plenty of cafés in summer. A Catalan tower keeps watch over the tiny marina.
Casa Deriu: Corso Vittorio Emanuele 59. Tel: 0785 377043. Open: Tue–Sun 11am–1pm & 5.30–8.30pm. Admission charge.

Capo Caccia and Grotta di Nettuno

This high wind-blown bluff points southwards into the Mediterranean and forms the northern tip of the Rada d'Alghero. The cliffs of Capo Caccia are one of Sardinia's bird breeding environments. The human interest lies in the **Grotta di Nettuno** (Grotto of Neptune), an immense cavern system that's open to the water. It is one of the most enjoyable and popular boat trips on this part of the coast.

Even in the 19th century tourists arrived to enjoy the awe-inspiring dimensions and veritable forest of stalactites and stalagmites. The scene is reminiscent of a swampy landscape, with mangrove roots poking up through the water. It has concretions ranging from spaghetti-thin strands to columns that measure metres in diameter, plus eccentric formations that defy gravity.

The caves were fitted with electric lighting in 1954 and a long staircase was carved into the rock face to allow access from the surface, so it's now possible to enter from above as well as by boat.
27km (17 miles) west of Alghero. Tel: 079 946540. Open: daily Apr–Sept 9am–7pm; Oct 9am–5pm; Nov–Mar 9am–4pm. Admission charge. Boat trips from the harbour at Alghero daily, Apr–Nov, weather permitting.

Castelsardo

Feudal fiefdom of the Doria family, Castelsardo vies with Bosa for the title of most attractive town in the northwest. Perhaps Castelsardo's setting on a dramatic coastal bay just has the edge!

The modern town with its pastel façades hangs like a fringe from the rocky knoll on which perches a tiny old town. The cobbled streets are now given over to tourism with an excellent range of handicrafts on offer, and, as you wander the streets, you'll see ladies making the straw and reed baskets for which the town is famed. Each one is produced by hand.

The Genoese Doria, who founded the town in the early 12th century, called their citadel Castelgenovese. When the Aragonese arrived they renamed it Castelaragonese, until finally the Piedmontese thought it better to give it the epithet Castelsardo or 'Sardinian Castle'. The tiny Doria fort on the peak houses the **Museo dell'Intreccio Mediterraneo**, offering background information on traditions of basketware.

There are a couple of churches within the town. Chiesa di Santa Maria sits in the lee of the upper citadel and displays a renowned 'Critu Neiddu' or Black Christ carved in the 13th century, while the Cattedrale di Sant'Antonio Abate has several pieces by the 'Maestro di Castelsardo', a painter whose real name and origins are not known.

Museo dell'Intreccio Mediterraneo: Tel: 079 471380. Open: summer Tue–Sun 9.30am–1pm & 3pm–midnight; winter Tue–Sun 9.30am–1pm & 3–8.30pm. Admission charge.

Chiesa di Michele Salvenero

Built in the 11th century in Pisan-Romanesque style as one element of a Vallambrosani monastery, much of

The tiny old town of Castelsardo

the church now lies in ruins. Its finest elements are the simple black-and-white façade, which was modified in the 13th century, and the original three semi-circular domes' apses, which can be viewed from the rear. Sadly, the complex sits surrounded by modern communications pylons and seems more than a little forlorn.

On route 597 between Sassari and Oschiri. Not open regular hours.

Chiesa San Pietro di Simbranos

Built in the early 12th century by the holy order of the Benedictines of Montecassino, the church is archetypal Pisan-Romanesque. However, as with Chiesa Michele Salvenero, the façade was updated with Gothic detail. The striped Pisan styling is very striking here and there is a wonderful carved stone relief above the door, depicting the abbot and two monks. An interesting modern addition in the interior is an altar carved from fossilised wood harvested from the petrified forest close by.

7km (4¼ miles) northwest of Pergugas. Not open regular hours.

Chiesa SS Trinita Saccargia

The Pisans founded the monastic order here in the 12th century, and the surrounding ruins indicate that it was a large complex during its heyday. The church was also ruined but underwent an enthusiastic renovation programme, funded by Diongi Scano in the 18th century, which is now frowned on by modern historians. An impressive site, with its Italianate portico offering welcome shade to summer visitors, and a rather over-heavy tower.

The highlight of the interior is the marvellous fresco cycle in the central apse that was painted when the church was newly completed. The scenes depict Christ Pantocrator (depicted as ruler of the Universe) with Mary and St Paul below and a third level featuring six episodes from the Bible including the Descent into the Underworld.

15km (9½ miles) southeast of Sassari. Open: 9am–1pm & 4–8pm. Admission free.

Coastal route Alghero–Bosa

There are some wonderful long-range views as you depart Alghero heading south along the coast. The road weaves in and out of wave after wave of rocky coves with surprisingly few beaches, the main stop being at La Speranza about 10km (6 miles) south of Alghero.

For lovers of nature, it's not so much what you see at eye level but what is wheeling above your head. About two-thirds of the way along the route the road wheels inland to where a community of griffon vultures has taken up residence in recent years. They truly are majestic creatures, with a wingspan of over 3m (around 10ft).

Cossione

This tiny and otherwise forgettable village is decorated with a selection of detailed wall frescoes and *trompe l'œil*, depicting folk leaning out of windows and dogs sleeping in doorways. The best is a full-scale recreation of a traditional *festa* complete with a procession in full traditional costume and a decorated ox cart.

Enoteca Tenute Sella e Mosca

The vineyard of Sardinia's best-known wine producer has been in business since 1899. The headquarters sit just outside Alghero. Here you can admire the 500 hectares (1,235 acres) of vines, enjoy a tour of the cellars during the summer and buy bottles of all the brands produced by Sella e Mosca in the *enoteca* or wine shop at below supermarket prices. Unfortunately they don't allow you to taste before you buy, but be assured that their finest full-bodied reds are certainly worth trying.

Loc I Piani, Alghero. Tel: 079 997700; www.sellaemosca.com. Tours: June–mid-Oct Mon–Sat 5.30pm. Enoteca open: mid-June–mid-Sept 8.30am–8pm; mid-Sept–mid-June 8am–1pm & 3–6.30pm. Admission free.

Monteleone Rocca Doria

Set atop a high rocky outcrop offering panoramic views over the Lago de Temo reservoir, Monteleone Rocca Doria was founded by the Genoese Doria family. The fortified settlement put up a valiant but ultimately unsuccessful resistance against the Aragonese, who promptly razed the castle to the ground. The journey up the switchback road offers much, and the village has some pretty renovated cottages and a couple of medieval chapels, but the overall effect doesn't

The coast road between Alghero and Bosa

Typical inland scenery in Sardinia

quite live up to expectations and the place has a somewhat modern and characterless feel.

Necropoli di Anghelu Ruju

Excavated at various times through the 20th century, the necropolis is the largest ancient burial ground on Sardinia, with over a dozen individual complexes to explore. Lovers of ancient history will find many highlights.

Tombs XXV and XXIX date from c. 3300–2900 BC and have a 'pozzetto' entrance that archaeologists believe pre-dates the open passage entrance of most of the tombs here. Finds indicate they were used by the Ozieri culture

that populated the lands in the north of the island before the development of Nuraghic culture.

Tomb XXX gave up some interesting artefacts that are closely related to the Beaker culture of the Iberian peninsula and the Balearic Islands just a little way west across the Mediterranean. However, the tomb is of typical Ozieri shape and style.

Tomb XXVIII, excavated in 1907, is the only curvilinear structure on the site and the carvings above the main portal have faint traces of carved bull horns on the pilasters; the bull is thought to have been a deity to these ancient peoples.

Tomb C has multiple rooms and is thought to have been carved to mimic a real home of the time. Finds here include a range of Ozieri and Copper Age (2900–2000 BC) items plus pottery from the Monte Claro culture that inhabited the northeastern part of the island.

Archaeologists believe from the range of artefacts found in the debris layer of Tomb II that it was used as a dwelling at one time. Both this and Tomb XX had finds from the Bonnanaro culture that dated to *c.* 1800 BC.

However, the most visually stunning tomb is that of XXbis, which is entered via a flight of steps down to the entrance portal, which has bull's head reliefs carved on the pilasters. Several Ozieri stone goddess sculptures were found here during the excavations. *9km (5½ miles) north of Alghero, on the Porto Torres road. Open: Apr–Oct 9am–7pm; Nov–Mar 9.30am–4pm. Admission charge.*

Necropoli di Pottu Codinu

The dómus de Janus or 'fairy homes' of Pottu Codinu were in constant use for burial rituals from the late Neolithic era (3500–2700 BC) to around 100 BC. The site encompasses nine tomb complexes, each with entrances facing towards the rising sun. Tomb VI is the most intricate, with seven chambers and niches, while Tomb I is the simplest, being linear in form with three connected chambers. Tomb V

Necropoli di Pottu Codinu

was used as a sheep and cattle pen until scientific study began in the late 1980s. Evidence of numerous fires indicates that the shepherd also rested overnight on site to protect his flock.

The finest objects uncovered during excavation were a Punic bell-cup in Tomb VI and an 46cm (18in) calcite statue of a 'Mother Goddess' of the Ozieri culture (3500–2800 BC).
35km (21½ miles) southeast of Alghero. Open: Tue–Sun 8.30am–12.30pm & 2.30–6.30pm. Admission charge.

Nuraghe di Palmavera

One of the most complete Nuraghic village complexes on Sardinia, the Palmavera site represents the whole gamut of ancient structures from the monumental to the domestic. This is also the first Nuraghic site to be scientifically excavated, by

A Tramelli in 1905. It was discovered to be a purely Nuraghic settlement from the very early days of the development of this unique culture and has been repeatedly studied as more information on these ancient peoples has come to light.

The primary *nuraghe* is a large circular tower built during the first phase of development (1500–900 BC), with an interior height of 7m (23ft) and a secondary adjunct, a smaller tower linked to the first by a small corridor. Around the *nuraghe* is a circular walled compound with four small towers and a larger circular 'meeting building', where the population would have got together to discuss important business and perhaps to hear cases of injustice or crime. The walls of the meeting house are lined with stone bricks with a

The ancient site of Nuraghe di Palmavera

A fortified medieval tower built by the Catalans stands next to the lighthouse in Porto Conte

cist (stone block box) and a carved limestone seat. In the centre is a pedestal, which archaeologists think was the seat for a stone statue. Over 50 stone huts surround the Nuraghic complex.

The nearest town to the *nuraghe*, Fertilia, was another of Mussolini's bright ideas, but the once monumental 1930s community buildings and hotels now have a rather careworn look. The outlet to the coastal lagoon and its reed beds promises much in the way of wildlife and there are the intriguing remains of an old Roman bridge to ponder on.

Fertilia (on the road to Porto Conte).
Open: Apr–Oct daily 9am–7pm;
Nov–Mar daily 9.30am–4pm.
Admission charge.

Porto Conte

Set in its own small bay between Alghero (*see pp92–4*) and Capo Caccia (*see p96*), the tiny resort of Porto Conte has a small selection of upmarket hotels and is overseen by a resilient Catalan tower. It was once the site of a Roman port.

Inland, **La Prigionette** nature reserve protects a number of creatures including wild boar and wild miniature horses brought from the Giara region further south.

La Prigionette: SP55 on the road to
Capo Caccia. Tel: 079 949060.
Open: Mon–Fri 8am–4pm, Sat, Sun
& holidays 9am–5pm. Admission free
with an identity card or passport.

Porto Torres

Founded by the Romans during their early dominion over the island, Porto Torres is still one of Sardinia's major ports and, it's fair to say, it isn't the prettiest spot on the island.

In the imperial era Turris Libisonsis, as the Roman city was called, transported cargoes from across the inland plain to the heart of the Empire. It suffered during the Vandal raids but continued to thrive into the Middle Ages when both Genoa and Pisa eyed it with envy. However, later Saracen raids and bouts of disease saw the end of the good times. Some of the ancient city was swallowed up by shifting sands, and, as Sassari (*see opposite*) increased in influence, Porto Torres declined.

On the seafront at the small port, a Catalan tower built in the wake of the Saracen raids still watches over proceedings. There's also a lone Roman column marking the end of the Karales (Cágliari) to Turris road. Vestiges of the Roman site lie around and about and are now collectively known as the Parco Archeologico (Archaeological Park). The major elements are the public baths, the Palazzo del Re Barbaro (entrance from the Museum, *see p128*), the necropolis, and the remains of the Roman bridge that once spanned the Rio Mannu, though this is covered in dust from passing trucks arriving from the modern ferry and container port just to the west.

The town's **Antiquarium Turritano** (Ancient Turris Museum) has many artefacts discovered during 20th-century excavations around town. The lower floor concentrates on small and mainly domestic objects, with several funerary collections, while on the upper floor mainly monumental remains are on show, including sections of mosaic floor found at the Central and Maetzke

Baths. Many fine pieces can also be seen in the Sanna Museum in Sassari.

Porto Torres lost its episcopal seat to Sassari in 1441, but the 11th-century Chiesa di San Gavino was Cattedrale di San Gavino until that time. It is one of the finest Romanesque churches on the island and unusual because it has an apse at each end. Despite the loss of status the church was expanded and a grand Calatan-Gothic portal was added in the 15th century. Within the complex you'll also be able to examine Roman and early Christian elements.
Antiquarium Turritano: Via Ponte Romano. Tel: 079 514433.
Open: Tue–Fri & Sun 9am–8pm, Sat 9am–4pm. Admission charge.

Sassari

Capital of northern Sardinia and the second-largest urban area on the island, Sassari is a fast-growing city, surrounded by monotone modern suburbs. The heart of the city is a vibrant living core, though getting in by car through a maze of one-way streets is a bit of a challenge.

The Sassari populace is feisty and independent, a legacy of the early days when they declared self-rule and negotiated separate agreements with the Genoese and the Catalans. The city fell into genteel decline from the 16th century until post-World War II renaissance, and today the 17th- and 18th-century palazzos are slowly being brought back to life.

In the heart of the maze of the medieval street plan is **Cattedrale di**

San Nicola (Duomo), a mainly 15th-century Gothic structure, with the most ornate façade on Sardinia. Added in the 18th century, it's almost like a stonemason's apprentice piece, with every centimetre carved and worked. Head inside for some magnificent frescoes or across the road to the small museum to view its liturgical treasures.

Further west, in the post-18th-century part of town, is the **Museo Nazionale G A Sanna** (G A Sanna National Museum), the north's premier history museum comprising excellent

The façade of the Duomo San Nicola in Sassari

archaeological artefacts, medieval galleries and a numismatic collection. Founded in 1887 as a Royal Collection, the original donation was sponsored by Senator Giovanni Antonio Sanna and opened on this site in 1931. There is a nice selection of *bronzetti* (miniature bronze statues), which are only surpassed by the number and quality in the Archaeological Museum in Cágliari (*see p44*), plus finds from all the major ancient sites in the area and from Roman Turris Libisonsis (Porto Torres) to the north. The coins are unique on Sardinia, with pieces dating from ancient Greek Sicily through Carthage, Rome and Byzantium to the kingdoms of Italy and Sardinia in the 18th century.

Lovers of military history should head to the **Museo della Brigata Sassari** (Sassari Brigade Museum), which charts the history and the battle honours of this famous outfit of World War I, though little of the information is in English.

Linking the medieval and neoclassical quarters are Corso Vittorio Emanuele, the main shopping street, and Piazza Italia, where the provincial headquarters is presided over by a statue of King Vittorio Emanuele II. There are excellent cafés around the square and along Via Roma in the direction of the Sanna Museum.

Sassari's main festival takes place on 14 August when giant candlesticks are carried around town from **Chiesa di Santa Maria di Betlem**. If you can't be

here then, the candlesticks are on show all year round in the church.

Cattedrale di San Nicola: Piazza del Duomo. Open: 9.30am–noon & 4–8pm.
Museo Nazionale G A Sanna: Via Roma 64. Tel: 079 272203. Open: Tue–Sun 9am–8pm. Admission charge.
Museo della Brigata Sassari: Piazza Castello. Tel: 079 233172. Open: Mon–Fri 9am–12.30pm & 2.30–4.30pm, Sat 9am–12.30pm. Admission free.
Chiesa di Santa Maria di Betlem: Piazza di Santa Maria. Open: 9am–1pm & 5–8pm.

Stintino

The beaches around this former fishing colony are some of the finest in the north, with long sandy stretches and the large lagoon of Stagno di Casaraccio offering excellent vistas and a place for flamingoes and other wild birds.

The population settled here as recently as the late 1800s when they were evicted from Asinara Island (*see p142*) just offshore.

A coastal tower stands just off La Pelosetta beach near Stintino

The central cone of the Nuraghe Santu Antine is over 20m (65ft) high

Torralba

A couple of historical attractions lie just south of this inland town. **Nuraghe Santu Antine** is an impressive ancient tower and helpful in showing the distinct development of the building over the generations. Started *c.* 1600 BC, the central cone reached over 20m (65ft) high and comprised three storeys. Surrounded by a compound, set with three round towers, it constitutes the archetypal form of the Nuraghic triangular complex. Climb up through the main tower to a viewing platform on what was the second floor. The remains of an associated village with its rounded stone huts lie around and just outside the central compound. The site was partially dismantled during the Roman era and again during the 19th century, when some of the

stone from the upper storey was carted off to Torralba for building projects.

The vale beyond Santu Antine is known as the 'Valley of the Nuraghe' for the many towers that dot the countryside. Visit the small **Museo Archeologico** (Archaeological Museum) in Torralba to view finds from the site.

Close by and now directly on the main north–south dual carriageway is the Pisan-Romanesque Chiesa di Nostra Signora di Cabu Abbas, which is another excellent example of the style.
Nuraghe Santu Antine: 3km (1³/₄ miles) south of Torralba. Open: 9am–8pm. Admission charge.
Museo Archeologico: Via Carlo Felice. Tel: 079 847298. Open: daily May–Oct 9am–8pm; Nov–Apr 9am–1pm & 3.30–6pm. Admission charge.

Drive: The northwest

This day tour takes you through some wonderful Mediterranean coastal and country scenery interspersed with an interesting variety of attractions that will keep your attention throughout the journey.

Time: 6 hours.

Distance: 175km (109 miles).

Start the day at Alghero.

1 Alghero
Take a stroll around the city walls and the Piazza Civica before enjoying the Museo Diocesano and the cathedral. *Head south on the coast road, signposted Bosa. Look out for griffon vultures here. After 45km (28 miles) you will reach a signpost for Bosa Marina to the right (2km/1¼ miles away).*

2 Bosa Marina
This is a small fine-sand beach, and a small fishing fleet ties up in the jetty that is watched over by a Catalan tower. *After enjoying the beach travel into Bosa town.*

3 Bosa
Bosa has a wonderful old town to explore. Stroll along Corso Vittorio Emanuele and walk the cobbled alleyways up to the castle or take in the river views from across the bridge. *Leave town by crossing the bridge and heading inland, following signs for Macomer. After 7km (4¼ miles) take the*

left turn signposted Pozzomaggiore and climb into the hills. There is a bypass around Pozzomaggiore village, so continue on in the direction of route 131 and carry on another 7km (4¼ miles) until you reach Cossione.

4 Cossione
Unremarkable Cossione is worthy of a halt because, like some other villages in Sardinia, it has beautified itself with some wonderful murals. The largest and most detailed are in the tiny square on the right in the centre of town. *Carry on in the direction you were originally travelling and you will drop down to meet the main 131 dual carriageway. Head north, but leave the road at the second junction signposted Nuraghe Santu Antine. From the 131 slip road turn left and the site is 500m (⅓ mile) on the right.*

5 Nuraghe Santu Antine
One of the finest examples of this unique Sardinian form of ancient architecture.

Return to the 131 but drive in the direction of Thies. Just before the village turn right up the rise and the Chiesa di San Pietro di Sorres stands on the right.

6 Chiesa di San Pietro di Sorres

Part of a still thriving monastic complex, Chiesa di San Pietro di Sorres is a triumphant example of Pisan-Romanesque architecture.

Return to the main road and travel through Thies. Five kilometres (3 miles) after the town take the left turn signposted Villanova Monteleone and Monteleone Rocca Doria, and continue for 14km (8¹/₂ miles) until the junction for Monteleone Rocca Doria appears on the right. Take this road and climb for 3km (1³/₄ miles) into the village.

7 Monteleone Rocca Doria

Yet another outpost of the medieval Doria family, Monteleone Rocca Doria lost its castle when the Aragonese arrived. The tiny village centre makes a pretty stroll, with a couple of Romanesque chapels and excellent views from the signposted panorama point.

Back on the main road, turn right towards Villanova Monteleone. After 6km (3³/₄ miles) stop at the burial site of Pottu Codinu on the right.

8 Necropoli di Pottu Codinu

Pottu Codinu is an important ancient burial site.

From Pottu Codinu carry on through Villanova Monteleone and take the twisting route back to Alghero.

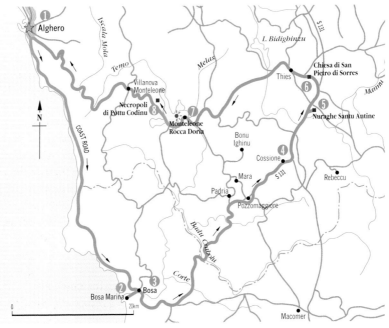

Walk: Alghero

The mostly pedestrian alleyways of Alghero's citadel make the perfect place for a stroll. This itinerary points out the highlights, but there's a wealth of detail to enjoy.

Time: 2½ hours. Distance: 2km (1¼ miles).

After parking the car in the car park on Via Garibaldi, the main coast road, make your way on the seafront promenade to the port in the shadow of the city walls.

1 Port

The port has its own fishing fleet and a range of pleasure craft. You could book a boat trip for later in the day.
Fronting the port side is the huge stone façade of the Bastione della Maddalena. Climb the steps on the right-hand side of the bastion, then turn right into the Piazza Civica.

2 Piazza Civica

This is the finest remaining medieval square on the island.
Look straight ahead as you enter the square. Above the café tables and canopies is the façade of Palazzo d'Albis.

3 Palazzo d'Albis

The most famed of the remaining historic buildings in the square, Palazzo d'Albis played host to Charles V when he visited Alghero in 1541.
After turning right into the square, walk across it (keeping Palazzo d'Albis on your left). Turn left along the second street, Via Carlo Alberto, and go on past the crossing

for Via Roma and Vicolo Adami until you reach the Chiesa di San Francesco.

4 Chiesa di San Francesco

The church is a fascinating mixture of Catalan-Gothic and Renaissance.
Return to Via Carlo Alberto and continue south. After passing four more left turns, you will reach Piazza Ginnasio, where you will find Chiesa di San Michele.

5 Chiesa di San Michele

This baroque church was built with money donated by local naval captain Gilbert Ferret. The foundation stone was laid in 1612.
Return down Via Carlo Alberto, then turn first right down Via Gilbert Ferret to reach Largo San Francesco.

6 Largo San Francesco

Torre di San Giovanni dominates the square and was once an integral element in the now demolished city wall.
Return down Via Gilbert Ferret and on past Via Carlo Alberto to Via Principe

Umberto. Turn right and walk on through Piazza del Teatro to Palazzo Machin on the left.

7 Palazzo Machin

The palazzo was built as the family home of Bishop Ambrogio Machin in the 17th century.

Pass by Machin and turn right at Via Roma. Then turn left along Via Maiorca and left again at Via G Manno. Museo Diocesano d'Arte Sacra is on the left.

8 Museo Diocesano d'Arte Sacra

The museum displays many liturgical objects and a few holy relics.

Turn left out of the museum into Piazza Duomo; the cathedral is on your left.

9 Cathedral

Enjoy the Catalan sacristy and the baroque marble altar.

Turn left out of the cathedral and climb the steps ahead to the top of the city walls.

10 Café Latino

The square directly ahead offers good views along the city walls. Then turn right to enjoy the finest views across the port and continue past Torre di Sant'Elmo until you reach the Café Latino for a well-deserved drink.

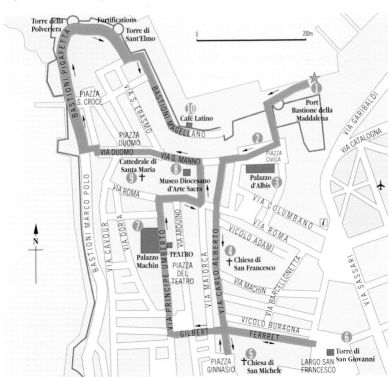

The northeast

In the early 1960s, Sardinia was put firmly on the tourist map when plans were announced for a 'super-resort', christened the Costa Smeralda. This new development would break the mould and create a haven for the super-rich. And what a location they chose: a boulder-strewn coastline with coves of golden sand and pristine waters that had been ignored for generations by the pastoral natives.

The northeast is much more than this one stretch of primped and preened holiday land. In fact, there is a whole swathe of delightful wild coast to explore. Further afield you will find a magnificent collection of ancient remains around the town of Arzachena, inland vineyards and oak forests, and you can take a fun ferry trip to the Maddalena Islands, to Isola Tavolara or across to Corsica, close to Sardinia in spirit yet part of the French nation.

Arcipelago di La Maddalena

Said to have been mentioned in Homer's *Odyssey*, the seven islands and numerous rocky islets of La Maddalena lie scattered out to sea just off the very northeastern corner of the island. Sardinians regarded them as insignificant and there was little human settlement here until the 18th century. Today the group is protected as the Parco Nazionale dell'Arcipelago di La Maddalena.

The island of La Maddalena, site of La Maddalena town, capital of the group, and Caprera are the two populated islands and both are mentioned later in this section (*see pp116 & 117*) but there are a rash of smaller islands that can only be reached by boat, and offer a wonderful opportunity to enjoy some unspoiled Mediterranean scenery. The islands are a yachting paradise and best seen when arriving by private yacht or group tour from La Maddalena town or from the mainland towns of Santa Teresa Gallura (*see pp124–6*) and Palau (*see pp122–3*).

Spargi is rocky but is the greenest of the islands, with wonderful sandy beaches on the south side, the best being Cala Corsara. Offshore from here, marine archaeologists found a Roman shipwreck, and some artefacts are now on display in the Museo dell'Arsenale at La Maddalena.

Budelli, Santa Maria and Razzoli make a semi-independent cluster of three islands to the northeast of Maddalena. Razzoli is known for its steep cliffs, but there is a sheltered anchorage at the bay of Cala Lunga on the southwest.

Santo Stefano, closest to the mainland, has an active NATO base, so much of the island is off-limits to the public.

The northeast

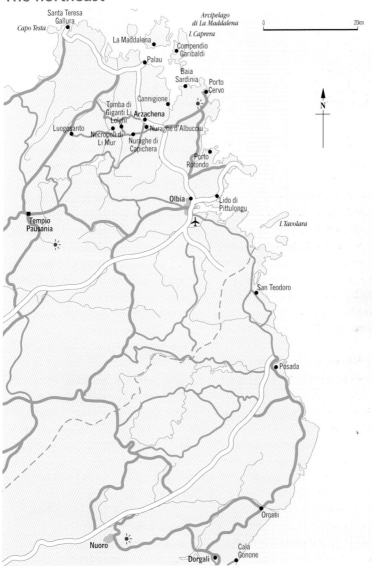

Cannigione marina

Arzachena

The money pouring into the Costa Smeralda region has certainly gentrified this bustling town. The streets have more than their fair share of design studios and furniture emporia, and several huge landscape garden centres sell olive trees and massive palms for the pristine gardens of the summer villas a few kilometres to the south.

Arzachena is also the focal point for trips to the high-quality ancient sites that are concentrated in the surrounding countryside. The information centre on the main road to the south of town has maps and fact sheets for each of the sites.

Baia Sardinia

Just on the northern edge of the Costa Smeralda, Baia Sardinia is a small resort set around a single sandy bay.

In summer the beach gets pretty crowded, but it offers a good balance of tourism infrastructure and nature.

Cala Gonone

One of the most dramatic resorts on Sardinia, Cala Gonone is located on the eastern coast, surrounded by a range of 900m (2,950ft) peaks and reached through a tunnel and down a steep switchback access road. The approach makes visitors feel they could be entering Shangri La and puts one in mind of the scene from *The Beach*, when the trio first discover the secret. However, Cala Gonone is known to more than a handful of folk and gets very busy in August.

A string of development has spread out around the main bay, and from here you can take boat trips to explore the dramatic cliffs and rock features along the coast, including the Grotte del Blue Marino and Cala di Lune.

Cannigione

This low-key one-street resort makes a good base for exploring the Costa Smeralda and the northeast. There are several sandy bays and a good-sized marina with lots of smaller local boats, dive companies and boat trips out around the coast.

There are no attractions as such here, but the atmosphere is genial.

Capo Testa

A dramatic and surreal landscape, the rocks at Capo Testa have been folded and twisted by the forces of nature and softened and rounded by the wind. Every angle offers myriad facets of golden rock undulating off into the distance with the waves crashing below at the water's edge. Clambering over the rocks is fun, or alternatively you can just sit and spend time contemplating the soothing shapes and shades.

If bare rock is a little too harsh a vista, just inland from the cape itself is a natural park area where rocks are intermingled with coastal shrub land and wild herbs.

Coddu Vecchiu and the Nuraghe di Capichera

The Coddu Vecchiu prehistoric tomb is the finest of the 'tombi giganti' of the Gallura region. The site has been especially useful to archaeologists because it has allowed them to study the development of Nuraghic funerary architecture over the centuries. The site started out as an *allée couverte* but was later updated into a 'giant's tomb' with the building of a grand portal. This entrance is fronted by a row of large flat rounded stones, carved with edging detail, the largest of which has a small arched entrance portal and a two-tier façade.

Immediately behind the façade is a small forecourt added when the tomb was expanded and modernised. The gallery grave is the oldest element in the complex. It is an immense enterprise, being over 10m × 4m (33ft × 13ft), with walls and roof made of basalt slabs, many of which remain in place to give a good overall impression of the original structure.

Archaeologists discovered a wealth of remains, including pottery from all eras of the burials, including some from the Copper Age Monte Claro culture (*c.* 2700–1800 BC), which is known to have inhabited only this small part of the island.

Giant tombs at Coddu Vecchiu

La Maddalena town curves round a sheltered harbour

Coddu Vecchiu is one element in an extended village complex that includes the Nuraghe di Capichera, a large but very overgrown conical tower. The ruined Demuro *nuraghe* is closer, at 200m (220yds) away from the tomb, but it is in a bad state of repair and considered to be in too dangerous a condition to enter.

Coddu Vecchiu: off the Arzachena– Luogosanto road. Tel: information office at Albucciu site (see p120) 0789 81537. Ticket office open: June–Aug 9am–7pm; Sept–May 9am–1pm & 4pm–sunset. Admission charge when ticket office manned (can combine ticket with two to five sites in the area).

Compendio Garibaldi

Italian revolutionary Giuseppe Garibaldi (1807–82) is a national hero on the mainland for his role in the military campaigns that led to the establishment of a united Italy. Between bouts of fighting he bought a huge tract of land on the island of Caprera in the Maddalena Archipelago and built Casa Blanca, which became his refuge. He enjoyed playing farmer, keeping chickens and goats, and staying out of the political melée. He died here and was interred in the grounds in keeping with his wishes. The house has many family artefacts and includes the general's deathbed, which has been left at the window where he requested it be moved so he could take in the view as he faded away.

Open: June–Sept Tue–Sun 9am–1.30pm & 4–7pm; Oct–May Tue–Sun 9am–1.30pm. Admission charge.

Dorgali

Lying on the border between the northern Gennargentu region and the plains of Orosei, Dorgali is a large town famed for its artisans and now a burgeoning centre for outdoor pursuits and adventure sports in the peaks to the south.

The town hangs around one long road snaking up a hillside. Along the route there are some excellent craft shops and traditional jewellers, so it's one of the best places in this part of the island to shop for genuine handicrafts.

Isola Tavolara

Set less than a kilometre (²/₃ mile) off the Sardinian shore, the limestone Isola Tavolara stands over 500m (1,640ft) high and dominates the surrounding coastline just to the south of Olbia. Sheer cliffs rise like a quiff above the water and sit in shimmering shallow azure waters. During the summer there are boat trips from Porto San Paolo, a tiny harbour on the mainland. You can while away a few hours on the Spiaggia Spalmatore, or take in a complete island circuit for views of the impressive cliff capes.

La Maddalena

Capital of the Maddalena Island, La Maddalena is a small town of pastel stucco façades set around a fine natural harbour. It is a bustling town full of excellent seafood restaurants and waterfront bars and is crowded with visitors from the main island on long summer days.

There are a couple of historical attractions. Visit the **Museo Archeologico Navale** (Naval Archaeological Museum) to view the exciting Roman remains discovered in

recent years in the waters off neighbouring Isola Spargi. The cargo of well-preserved amphorae has been set in a recreated section of hull showing how the vessel would have been loaded for its fateful trip. The **Museo Diocesano** (Diocese Museum) contains two silver candlesticks, a handwritten letter and a cross dedicated to the church by Nelson.

Museo Archeologico Navale: Strada Panoramica, Loc Mongiardino. Tel: 0789 790660. Open: Tue–Sun 8am–2pm. Admission charge. Museo Diocesano: Via Barone Manno. Open: 10.30am–1pm & 3–8pm summer only. Admission free.

Lido di Pittulongu

Pittulongu is the place where Olbia's young and beautiful head on summer evenings and at the weekends.

However, though there are watersports providers and several well-established bars, the beach is disappointing by Sardinian standards. Come for the atmosphere but do not expect to get much sand to yourself.

Necropoli di Li Mur

The burial ground of Li Mur is the most archaeologically significant of the Arzachena region's many ancient sites. Examination of the remains suggests that the ground was considered sacred by the unique 'megalithic circle' culture, thought to be a separate people from those of the Ozieri culture to the west.

The site, discovered in 1939, consists of a series of dolmen cists, small stone-

Necropoli di Li Mur

lined burial cells that were surrounded by several concentric circles of upright stone slabs that would contain earth to protect the body or skeleton inside. So, in effect, the site would have looked like a series of large mounds with a diameter of around 5m (16½ft) each. The final edging circle included a menhir (tall upright stone), perhaps to identify the person inside or to protect the body from evil. The inner stone chambers and some sets of concentric circles can clearly be seen here at Li Mur.

Archaeologists found the remains of several ancient containers on site, which perhaps held food for the journey into the afterlife. Grave goods also include a soapstone cup, flint blades, hatchets, stones with holes carved through them and hand weapons. Everything indicates a high quality of workmanship.

Tel: information office at Albucciu site (see p120) 0789 81537. Ticket office open: June–Aug 9am–7pm; Sept–May 9am–1pm & 4pm–sunset. Admission charge when ticket office

manned (can combine ticket with two to five sites in the area).

Nuoro

Capital of the province that covers much of the Gennargentu (*see pp136–42*), Nuoro has a reputation as an insular place, and as you approach the city from any direction it is easy to understand why. It would have been a difficult journey from any direction before the invention of motorised transport, and even today the main signpost for the city centre points down a one-way street where traffic moves in the wrong direction. It also disowned its most famous modern daughter Grazia Deledda when she wrote a few things it was not too pleased with, though reconciliation was reached before her death and she is buried in the small church of Nostra Signora della Solitudine in the city.

However, once you break through these minor barriers, it is certainly a worthwhile city in which to spend an hour or two. Nuoro acts as a cultural headquarters for traditional crafts, arts and the Sardinian language.

Head to the **Museo della Vita e delle Tradizioni Sarde** (Museum of Sardinian Life and Tradition) for one of the island's most comprehensive collections of traditional costumes along with gold and silver jewellery and adornments. Craft items include good examples of traditional country furniture, rugs and textiles, and musical instruments. This is an excellent place to get to grips with the island's complicated and fascinating traditional culture.

The **Museo Archeologico Nazionale** (National Archaeological Museum) has recently been spruced up in the newly renovated Palazzo Asproni. The collection includes finds from all across Nuoro province, and the galleries continue to expand as the museum settles into its new home.

The city does not spend all its time looking backwards. The **Museo d'Arte Provincia di Nuoro** (Nuoro Provincial Art Museum) or MAN is one of Italy's most celebrated modern art galleries and hosts an ever-changing range of avant-garde exhibitions.

Though Grazia Deledda became a *persona non grata*, another famous native author, Salvatore Satta, has always been a favoured son. Satta's birthplace is now a museum and the city has named a square after him that is decorated with commemorative statues and sculptures.

For once, churches do not get major billing. Nuoro's neoclassical Cattedrale di Santa Maria della Neve was inaugurated in 1853 – it is, however, a triumph of size over taste.

Head to Corso Garibaldi, a cobbled pedestrian artery through the heart of the city, for shopping and cafés.
Tourist office: Corso Garibaldi.
Tel: 0784 30083.

Landscape around Nuoro

Museo della Vita e delle Tradizioni Sarde: Via Antonio Mereu 56. Tel: 0784 257035. Open: mid-June–Sept daily 9am–8pm; Oct–mid-June daily 9am–1pm & 3–7pm. Admission charge.
Museo Archeologico Nazionale: Via Mannu 1. Tel: 0784 33793.
Open: Tue–Sun 9am–1.30pm & 3–6pm. Admission charge.
Museo d'Arte Provincia di Nuoro: Via Satta 15. Tel: 0784 252110; www.museoman.it. Open: Tue–Sun 10am–1pm & 4.30–8.30pm. Admission charge.

Nuraghe d'Albucciu

This is still one of the finest of Sardinia's many *nuraghi*, though the structure has collapsed in on itself and was once much larger and more complicated. The fun for the visitor is to be able to climb up inside the tower via a stone staircase to a plateau area on what would have been the first floor. For the scientists, Albucciu is a continued source of valuable information on Nuraghic building methods and lifestyle and has been the focus of many scientific studies.

The fortress is an irregular rectangle with rounded corners and has been built using the natural topography, incorporating several large outcrops and boulders. The interior has several ground-floor chambers, some of which were used for human habitation. Archaeologists believe that the tower was used by the community as a place of safety in times of danger and would not have been lived in full time. During excavations, artefacts have been found in several layers, indicating different generations of inhabitants: these include decorated bowls with handles, a highly ornate bronze votive dagger, flint blades and domestic pottery.
Tel: information office 0789 81537.
Ticket office open: June–Aug 9am–7pm; Sept–May 9am–1pm & 4pm–sunset. Admission charge when ticket office manned (can combine ticket with two to five sites in the area).

Olbia

The town of Olbia sits on a lovely natural inlet, but in many ways this has been its downfall. Natural inlet also means natural harbour, and with its location closest to the Italian mainland it made perfect sense to develop a port here. Olbia grew rapidly in the late 20th century on the back of its trade connections and the building of an international airport close by. It is the nearest large conurbation to the Costa Smeralda, but it is not the most attractive town on the island.

The modern structure sits directly on the ancient town of Terranova Pausania founded, it is thought, by the Carthaginians. The city flourished under the Romans, but in the wake of Rome's collapse and a sacking by the Vandals the population moved to a site named Fausania though this was also in decline after the first millennium.

The main attraction of the town is the Chiesa di San Simplicio, originally

11th century, but expanded in the following century when the church was upgraded into a cathedral (until 1503). The granite façade is a worthy example of the northern Italian Romanesque style and there are numerous old tombstones in the interior, plus many old milestones rescued from the Terranova Pausania–Karales (Cágliari) road. *Tourist office: Via Alessandro Nanni 39. Tel: 0789 21453.*

Orosei

Set in the heart of a fertile coastal plain, Orosei presides over the sublime beaches of the Golfo di Orosei to the east, and a series of low-key resorts that sit sheltered under aromatic pine trees, some of the best being around La Caletta to the north.

Little changed, as yet, by the arrival of tourism, the old town is a knot of narrow cobbled alleyways that seem to have more than their fair share of churches, many set around the town's main square, the shady Piazza del Popolo, with its cafés and bars. The main place of worship is the Cattedrale di San Giacomo, a lime-washed neoclassical basilica. Though this is the biggest church, it is not, however, the most interesting. Across the square is the Chiesa Sas Animas (the entrance

The pretty tiled dome of Chiesa di San Paolo in Olbia

A view over Palau towards Maddalena Island

is around the other side on Piazza Sas Animas), an earlier and simpler edifice, where the old folk gather on the seats outside for a chat in the evening shade.

Across Piazza Sas Animas you will see the remains of Prigione Vecchia, the rather careworn medieval tower, the last remaining vestige of a larger castle, and down the alleyway to the right is the baroque chapel of Chiesa del Rosario.

Palau

The jumping-off point for ferries from the mainland to the Maddalena Islands, Palau is a lively town with some good shopping and dining. The many pastel façades climbing up the hill from the port look beautiful from a distance but are rather modern and boxy close up: evidence that the town has grown

quickly over the last few years. However, at least some attempt has been made to maintain the overall low-rise Mediterranean-style vistas.

The town has a large pleasure port that swells with visiting yachts in summer, and from here you can take boat tours around the islands. The ferry is a cheap and regular (every 15 minutes) service that drops you right in the heart of La Maddalena town (*see p117*) and runs from early morning to around midnight.

If you notice more than a smattering of American being spoken around the town, it is NATO personnel from the base at Santo Stefano making a mainland visit. Above the town the sandstone 19th-century citadel of **Fortezza di Monte Altura** is another, older defensive structure.

Fortezza di Monte Altura: Tel: 335 1276849. Open: daily June–Aug 9am–noon & 5–8pm; Sept–May 10am–1pm & 3–7pm. Admission charge.

Porto Cervo

'Capital' of the Costa Smeralda, Porto Cervo is one of the Mediterranean's most upmarket resorts. The super-rich do not just holiday here: they own property here – so it is a mini-state within a state with its own by-laws and resident 'rules and regulations'.

The roll-call of owners reads like *Forbes* magazine meets *Who's Who*, with European royalty, industrial magnates and a smattering of celebrities. They come to spend the summer among like-minded people enjoying fine restaurants and sailing off in their yachts to some offshore anchorage away from the riffraff.

The apartments and villas are all set in ample beautifully landscaped gardens, and the communal greenery such as roadside verges is tended impeccably. The shopping is an amalgam of designer names, chic galleries and yacht 'supermarkets' for those who have a spare £5 million or so burning a hole in their pockets.

In season, Porto Cervo is full of nautical atmosphere, but it's pretty much empty at other times, when one might wonder what all the fuss is about.

The northeast

A yacht leaves Porto Cervo

Porto Rotondo

The smaller and slightly cheaper neighbour of Porto Cervo, Porto Rotondo is actually the more attractive of the two, more 'villagey' and cosier, set around a small circular bay. Technically it is outside the strict boundaries of the Costa Smeralda, but the uninitiated cannot tell, since the styling and the road signs are the same.

Posada

One of the prettiest towns on the eastern coast, Posada's pastel-hued cottages tumble down a hill below the sturdy medieval Castello de Fava or Bean Castle (*see panel on p125*), creating a picture-perfect panorama. Though there are few individual attractions, the old town is an atmospheric place to stroll and browse.

San Teodoro

One of the rising stars of Sardinian tourism, San Teodoro attracts the young and fashionable Italian crowd for its beaches (some without road access), watersports and nightlife.

Santa Teresa Gallura

Sardinia's most northerly town, Santa Teresa Gallura hugs the rugged pink cliffs close to Capo Testa and points the way

The view down the coast from the Castello de Fava in Posada

The beach at Santa Teresa Gallura

north to Corsica. You can see the white cliffs of the French sister island only 15km (9½ miles) away.

There has been settlement here since ancient times, but the town received a boost when it became the

WHAT'S IN A NAME

Castello de Fava gets its name from one of the most famous incidents in Sardinian history. During one of their regular raids, Arab forces laid siege to the castle where the local townspeople had taken refuge. As time went on, food supplies ran short, and, with no respite in sight, the future looked bleak. Then someone had a bright idea! Feed the last supplies of food, a handful of fava beans, to a pigeon and then arrange for it to land in the Arab camp so that when they open the bird up it gives the impression that the castle has ample supplies. The plan worked, the Arabs gave up and the town was saved.

base for anti-pirate patrols under the House of Savoy in the early 1800s. It is a relatively modern town centre with post-World War II outskirts. History has not been totally excised, however. The 16th-century Torre di Longonsardo sits on a headland between the port inlet and Spiaggia Rena Blanca, the town's beach.

Today, the ferry crosses the Bocche di Bonifacio strait several times each day. You could take a day trip to Bonifacio, a fantastic medieval citadel town (journey time 90 minutes), or at the head of the inlet there is a modern marina where you could hire a boat.

The town is famed for its coral, and there are more than enough shops selling a vast selection of the deep pink stone. Part of the town centre is traffic free and there is a spacious modern town square where adults sit at one of a selection of cafés while the kids play safely within earshot.

Tempio Pausania

Often bypassed in the rush along the coast to the north or the dual carriageway to the south, Tempio Pausania sits in rolling hills, surrounded by vineyards and cork oaks. This region is famed for Vermentino, the soft, fruity white wine that goes perfectly with the fresh Sardinian seafood. You will be able to buy it at numerous vineyards.

Founded by the Romans, Tempio Pausania was owned by the powerful Massa family in medieval times, until the arrival of the Spanish. Granite is the building material of choice here and gives a curious monochrome feel to the old streets. The town is dominated by the grey Cattedrale di San Pietro, with 15th-century antecedents but a 19th-century façade. It may be something in the local water, but in the 20th century the town has been the birthplace of three internationally recognised opera singers.

Tomba di Giganti di Li Lolghi

Set at the summit of a small mound, the giant's tomb at Li Lolghi is beautifully sited, and the eye is immediately drawn to the monolithic stele at the centre of the façade, which rises to 3.75m (12¼ft). Unfortunately, it was broken when it fell many

centuries ago, so it is not as singularly impressive as the stele at Coddu Vecchiu (*see pp115–16*) close by.

Behind the façade, in the body of the tomb, you can get good views of the chamber because the roof stones are not *in situ*. Archaeologists now suggest that the site was extended three times from the original *allée couverte* design as the people became more sophisticated and wealthier. The most central and oldest part of the tomb is a 3.7m (12ft) long and 0.95m (3ft) wide cist (stone box), which contained either the bodies or skeletons of the incumbents. The long corridor, added in a subsequent expansion, is wider than the original cist.

The grave goods found also confirm at least two stages of development, with the earliest dating from the Early Bronze Age (1800–1600 BC) Bonnanaro culture, along with the later Middle Bronze Age (1600–1300 BC) Nuraghic culture, indicated by shards of ceramics.

It is now thought by modern scientists that the name Li Lolghi, from the Gallurian dialect *lalgi*, meaning 'rings', may have been the first modern name for the nearby Necropoli di Li Mur (*see pp117–18*) and that over the years the two got mixed up.

Tel: information office at Albucciu site (see p120) 0789 81537.
Ticket office open: June–Aug 9am–7pm, Sept–May 9am–1pm & 4pm–sunset.
Admission charge when ticket office manned (can combine ticket with two to five sites in the area).

Tomba di Giganti Li Lolghi

Drive: The north coast

Ease your way from west to east on a journey that takes in all the major attractions along the route. This trip also offers some major souvenir hunting opportunities.

Time: 8 hours.

Distance: 180km (112 miles).

Start your journey in Alghero.

1 Alghero

The Sardinian headquarters of the Aragonese, Alghero is still the most Spanish of Sardinia's towns.
Leave Alghero on the road north following signposts to Porto Torres. After 10km (6 miles) you will find the ancient site of Anghelu Ruju on the left.

2 Necropoli di Anghelu Ruju

This is an excellent example of an ancient burial site.
Continue on the road to Porto Torres. After a further 26km (16 miles) you will reach this important port town.

3 Porto Torres

Porto Torres was an important Roman settlement and there are still some sections of the ancient town to explore. The Archaeological Museum sits beside one of them, the Palazzo del Re Barbaro, and contains an excellent range of finds. Take time also to see the 11th-century Chiesa di San Gavino, once the city cathedral.

Leave Porto Torres travelling east along the coast in the direction of Castelsardo. The road runs directly along the long narrow beaches and you may see surfers enjoying the waves that can be quite challenging early and late in the year. After 30km (18¹/2 miles) Castelsardo comes into view across the bay. Drive through the modern town and up to the citadel.

4 Castelsardo

The oldest part of Castelsardo sits atop a high coastal bluff and was fortified by the Doria family, a powerful medieval Genoese dynasty. Their castle claims the highest ground and below is a tiny historic enclave that is a delight to explore. Castelsardo is famed for its basketware.
Leave Castelsardo on the landward route south (following the main road through town). Four kilometres (2¹/2 miles) from the town there is a junction with a left turn signposted Santa Teresa Gallura. The road runs inland past the Costa

Paradiso until you reach the town after 70km (43 miles).

5 Santa Teresa Gallura

Much of Santa Teresa Gallura is 18th century. The centre is a grid of attractive streets surrounding a large main square and you can enjoy a spot of shopping: coral is a speciality of the town (the industry is now well controlled but coral has been greatly overharvested from the Mediterranean). You could also take the ferry to Corsica from here.

Leave town to the west following the road signposted to Capo Testa. After 5km (3 miles) you will reach the car park.

6 Capo Testa

The rocky Capo Testa is one of the natural highlights of Sardinia, so take time to scramble over the rocks to take in all the angles.

Return to Santa Teresa Gallura and leave along the main road as if returning to Castelsardo. After 2km (1¹/₄ miles) take the left turn to Palau, a journey of 25km (15¹/₂ miles).

7 Palau

Palau is a pleasant port town with no real attractions, but stroll around the port or along the main street with its range of shops.

The ferry for La Maddalena runs every 15 minutes from Palau and takes around 20 minutes to cross the narrow straits.

8 La Maddalena

The best views of La Maddalena are from the water, where the pastel façades glow in the late afternoon sun.

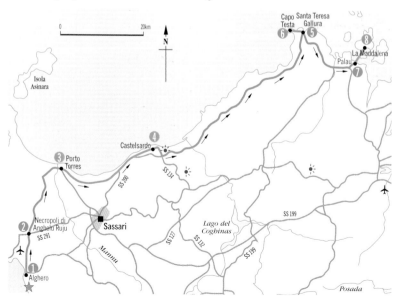

Drive: Costa Smeralda

This whole section of the northeast coast north of Olbia is basking in the publicity generated by the Costa Smeralda. This 'concept' region occupies just a small stretch of this incredibly beautiful coastline but brings more than a touch of glamour to this part of the Mediterranean. Travel along the coast, taking in the celebrity haunts before ending the journey with a short ferry trip to Sardinia's northeastern tip.

Time: 5 hours.

Distance: 65km (40 miles).

1 Porto Rotondo

Begin the journey here. Just outside the official boundary of the Costa Smeralda, this is a secondary port for the multi-million-dollar gin palaces that tie up in the jetties. It is a pretty natural curved bay with a collection of pastel villas dotting the hillside.
Leave Porto Rotondo on the main road towards Olbia. After 3km (1¾ miles)

turn right and after another 3km (1¾ miles) right again following signs to Porto Cervo. The road drops down to the coast, then swings inland. You will see signs for Portisco on the right.

2 Portisco

Portisco is the smallest yachting harbour along this stretch of coast and looks out across the Golfo di Cugnana back towards Porto Rotondo.
Climb back out of the port and turn left at the top of the hill. At the next junction turn right following signs for San Pantaleo.

3 San Pantaleo

San Pantaleo is a pretty village of stone houses, with some nice cafés. It is surrounded by the most sublime landscape: an undulating land of huge granite boulders and verdant low-growing brush land.
In the middle of San Pantaleo the

road splits. Take the right-hand turn signposted Porto Cervo and Arzachena. After 4km (2¹/₂ miles) there will be a junction on the right to Porto Cervo. Take this for the 14km (8¹/₂-mile) cross-country trek to the port.

4 Porto Cervo

Porto Cervo is the flagship development of the Costa Smeralda. It is a small town of large mansions and luxurious apartment complexes combined with upmarket shopping and a large marina.

Leave Porto Cervo by taking the coast road north signposted Baia Sardinia. After 6km (3³/₄ miles) turn right at the T-junction to take the road to Baia Sardinia beach.

5 Baia Sardinia

Baia Sardinia is the first place on the trip with some sand and somewhere for the children to paddle.

From Baia Sardinia follow signs for Arzachena. After 8km (5 miles) there is a junction to the right, signposted Cannigione, and after 3km (1³/₄ miles) another into the resort.

6 Cannigione

Cannigione is a pretty resort spread out around several sandy bays and with a small, more workaday marina than on the Costa.

Return out of Cannigione the same way you entered and drive to the roundabout for the Arzachena bypass. Follow signs into the centre of the town.

The old church in San Pantaleo

7 Arzachena

Arzachena is the base for the tour of several important ancient sites. The information office is on the outskirts of town on the right.

Travel on through the town and continue following signs to Palau. You will reach the town after 12km (7¹/₂ miles).

8 Palau

Once at Palau, the main road leads through the town to the port, with ferries for La Maddalena. Turn right just before the port to park for a trip into the town, which has some good shopping.

Ferries for La Maddalena depart from Palau every 15 minutes throughout the day. Take the car or cross as a foot passenger.

9 La Maddalena

The town of La Maddalena is a lovely place to stroll.

The founding of the Costa Smeralda

'Costa Smeralda is one of the most prestigious and pristine resorts in the world. We are honored to continue the vision and stewardship of the Costa Smeralda founder, Prince Karim Aga Khan, who first unwrapped the emerald coast's beauty. Our hope is to be the vehicle through which the ultimate dreams and desires of the Sardinian people are finally realised.

No one can truly own the Costa Smeralda. Rather, it owns you.'
Tom Barrack,
Chairman and CEO of Colony Capital
(*www.colonycapital.com*)

These were the words of Barrack as the ink from his signature was drying on the deal that gave his real estate investment firm a controlling interest

The interior of the Costa Smeralda

in the business side of the Costa Smeralda. He has turned around the Savoy Group, Raffles Hotel in Singapore and a host of upmarket properties since the 1980s. Colony Capital was the biggest thing to hit the property equity market in the late 20th century, making 21 per cent annually on its global portfolio.

What this property mogul was buying into is one of the most unusual tourist developments in the world, the dream of one man that has turned this part of Sardinia into a summer haven for Europe's movers and shakers.

Karim Aga Khan IV was a debonair playboy who had just inherited his title. He moved in an elite social circle and looked around for somewhere he and his super-rich pals could call a playground, somewhere they could put their stamp on and call home for a few weeks every summer. He came to view this tiny stretch of the northeastern coast with its sublime beaches, incredible topography and coves suitable to moor their super yachts and liked what he saw. He bought up 5,000 hectares (12,355 acres) in 1962 and formed Corsorzio Costa Smeralda (meaning Emerald Coast) to manage the resort.

The Italian super-rich already loved it here, setting sail from the mainland Italian coast. They were certainly willing to throw a few lire in to create their own super-club. The Aga Khan worked personally with the famous Italian architects Busiri-Vici and Vietti to plan the site and create a 'village', which includes a church as well as fantastic marina facilities, shopping opportunities featuring the best designer names, and fine dining, so that no one needed to leave the coast and enter the real world. Villa owners became members of the consortium, with voting rights and a say in exactly what goes on around town. This is not a public venue; this is a privately owned tiny enclave where visitors are limited to just four hotels.

The consortium protects the interests of the members and the brand name and reputation of the Costa Smeralda. It vets all new development and also organises a full social calendar, including rallies and regattas, and other activities to keep the members happy.

AGA KHAN IV

Prince Karim El Husseini is the 49th Imam or spiritual leader of the Ismaili Muslims, the second-largest Shia sect. His family pass the title on through the generations because they are direct blood descendants of the prophet Muhammad. The present Aga Khan was born in 1936 in Geneva and brought up in Kenya. Educated in Switzerland before gaining his degree at Harvard, he succeeded to the title on his father's death in 1957.

Tour: Ancient sites of Arzachena

The concentration of ancient sites in the countryside surrounding this busy town has allowed archaeologists a rich seam of both structures and artefacts to study. From these they have built a picture of the lifestyle of the Gallurian cultures that called the place home over the generations. The same route could make a lovely day-long walk, but do take plenty of water and snacks, and wear comfortable shoes.

Time: 3 hours.

Distance: 24km (15 miles).

Park at the information centre at the Nuraghe d'Albucciu site, a couple of kilometres (1¼ miles) south of Arzachena. After buying your tickets, make your way through the underpass to emerge at the site.

1 Nuraghe d'Albucciu

The Nuraghe d'Albucciu has been of prime importance to archaeologists in their attempt to unravel the lifestyle of the Nuraghic people. Although the tower has collapsed in on itself, the interior structure is impressive, with a stone staircase leading to an upper platform.

Return to the car park and walk up the lane at the left-hand side of the information office. After 1,500m (1 mile), over fields and through rocks in the latter part, you will reach the site of the Tempietto Malchittu.

2 Tempietto Malchittu

The site consists of several well-spaced buildings, but the highlight is the small temple itself, a small horseshoe-shaped building with a wall and entrance door. Unfortunately, a cache of ceramics found here by archaeologists was smashed by a holm oak tree that had grown up through the structure in recent decades.

The Tomba di Giganti di Coddu Vecchiu

From the tomb take the road right for a couple of hundred metres/yards and there will be a signpost to the Nuraghe di Capichera.

4 Nuraghe di Capichera

This *nuraghe* is less well preserved than d'Albucciu but is certainly worth a short visit.

Return along the route past Coddu Vecchiu to the main road. Turn left towards Luogosanto for 1,500m (1 mile), then turn right, following signposts for Li Lolghi. The road is a dirt track but causes no problems for 2WD vehicles. After 2.5km (1½ miles) you will see the site on your left.

5 Tomba di Giganti di Li Lolghi

On a finer site than Coddu Vecchiu, set on the crest of a small hill, this smaller structure is less well preserved.

From the car park at Li Lolghi, turn right and then right again 200m (220yds) beyond to climb the hill through boulder-strewn farmland to Necropoli di Li Mur.

6 Necropoli di Li Mur

This is the finest example of dolmen cist burial sites on Sardinia, where visitors can easily perceive the circular stone structure that protected the stone funerary chamber.

From the entrance to the site head right and then right again at the T-junction. After 5km (3 miles) there is a roundabout. Take the right turn to the centre of Arzachena.

Return to the information office and pick up the car. Turn left out of the car park to a large roundabout, then take the first exit right, following signs for Palau and Santa Teresa Gallura. Continue, following roundabouts until there is a left turn for Luogosanto. Take this left turn and after 2km (1¼ miles) there is a left turn signposted Tomba di Giganti di Coddu Vecchiu.

3 Tomba di Giganti di Coddu Vecchiu

The best preserved of the Tomba di Giganti or giants' tombs, named after the huge granite slabs that have been carefully worked and placed to create an impressive façade. The main arched stele is beautifully worked and the tomb chamber has many original wall, floor and ceiling stones still in place.

Getting away from it all

Arrive in August and you would be forgiven for thinking there was nowhere on Sardinia where you could escape the crowds, but you would be wrong. The sunbathers flock to the coastal resorts, but the countryside and especially the mountains in the east are rarely targeted. The hills have the added advantage of being a couple of degrees cooler in high summer (they are high enough for snow in the winter) and there is always something pleasing to discover on your travels.

But getting away from it all is as much about timing as it is about geography. Visit Sardinia in the warming days of late spring or the balmy early autumn and you will find the whole island seems like your personal playground; the roads are free of traffic and the beaches delightfully empty.

The following areas are 'the road less travelled' whatever time of year you choose to visit.

The Barbagia and Gennargentu

Sardinia's most dramatic and challenging regions lie in the mountainous east. In times past, this was the place where the natives would retreat in the wake of foreign invasions and from where freedom fighters would set out to raid the coastal towns that were under the domination of, say, the Catalans or the Piedmontese.

The first thing that has to be said about the east is that the landscapes are both dramatic and incredibly beautiful. Row after row of forested peaks take on

a faint blue cast in the morning light and mellow in the glow of the sunset. The shepherd is king of the mountains and flocks roam over every hill and vale. The melodic jangling of bells rings around the mountains, but they do not just hang around sheep's necks: they signal approaching cow herds too. Feral pigs and wild boar also roam, grubbing for seeds and tubers or squabbling over the last spot in the muddy wallow.

The Gennargentu is the highest region in Sardinia. The series of peaks reaching just over 1,800m (5,900ft) are hardly in the same league as the Alps, but their rocky ridges put you in mind of a more verdant big sky country in the United States, with occasional rock towers standing sentinel-like above the rest. To the west and south is a series of rolling hills known as the Barbagia, the geographical heart of Sardinia.

There are over 50 communities scattered across the landscape and numerous natural and man-made treasures to find as you explore the twisting mountain roads. Notable natural features include the Flumendosa valley that wends its way south through the peaks, punctuated by impressive waterfalls and natural lakes, and the peaks in the far east that drop into the sea in a series of cliffscapes punctuated by hidden coves.

The families of this region have perhaps the purest Sardinian bloodline and over the centuries have developed into close-knit, hardy and fiercely independent communities, with a reputation for insularity.

There are different rules here. A life dominated by poverty, crippling land rents and sheep rustling is still within living memory. Locals carry rifles as a matter of course and family feuds started by the smallest slights have been passed down through the generations. This region was also the heartland of

Fissure in the Gennargentu

Girasole beach, Arbatax

the rash of celebrity kidnappings that took place on Sardinia in the 1980s and early 1990s.

As a tourist you would be hard pressed to notice any undercurrents of this brooding emotion as you tour the region. There is as much civility to foreigners as in the rest of the island, and you can be sure that, whatever the reputation, you are not stepping back into a Sardinian Wild West.

This journey is as much about the landscape as it is about the destination, but a few towns and villages certainly deserve a mention in dispatches.

Arbatax

This small town set in a verdant plain amid the mountains welcomes ferries from the Italian mainland to its workaday port. It is not worth a special visit, but it is a good pit stop on your tour, and, if you are happening to be passing, you can head down behind the docks to view the island-renowned 'red rocks' that sit just offshore.

To the north are some excellent sandy stretches if you want to take a beach break for a while.

Aritzo

Before the invention of electric refrigeration the townsfolk of Aritzo made a living selling snow in town markets around the island. Today it is the heart of chestnut country and has a pleasing core of historic buildings, including **Chiesa di San Michele**

Archangelo, which dates back to the 11th century. The **Museo Etnografico** (Ethnographic Museum) is packed with old farming implements and the usual paraphernalia. The old photographs showing the town and the lifestyles of a bygone age are fascinating.

Museo Etnografico: Tel: 0784 629223. Open: Tue–Sun 10.30am–1pm & 4.30–7pm. Admission charge.

Belví

This tiny village plays host to the only **Museo di Scienze Naturali** (Museum of Natural History) on Sardinia. The galleries are crammed with mineral geodes, seashells, butterflies, insects and a range of stuffed animals and birds. The hills around the town have numerous ancient dómus de Janus.

Museo di Scienze Naturali: Via Roma 17. Tel: 0784 629467. Open: June–Sept Tue–Sun 9am–noon & 2–7pm; Oct–May Tue–Sun 9am–noon & 3–6pm. Donations accepted.

Désulo

The **Museo Etnografico** (Ethnographic Museum) is one of the finest on the island and is found in the former home of poet Antioco Casula (1878–1957), who wrote his works in the Sardinian language. The lower floors have some fascinating displays relating to the staple industries of the area, including shepherding, woodcarving and weaving. The traditional costumes of the women of the region are very colourful, so try to

time your visit to coincide with a summer festival (*see p29*).

Museo Etnografico: Casa Montanaru. Tel: 0784 619624. Open: summer Tue–Sun 10am–1pm & 4.30–7.30pm; winter Tue–Sun 10am–1pm & 4–7pm. Admission charge.

Isili

Head here for the **Museo per l'Arte del Rame e del Tessuto** (Museum of Copper and Weaving) housed in the well-renovated 17th-century monastery. The collection has excellent examples of traditional rugs and blankets plus displays showing how copper was worked to produce useful household objects.

Close by is the **Nuraghe Is Paras**, which was developed over several generations and has fortifications built during the early first millennium.

Museo per l'Arte del Rame e del Tessuto: Via San Giuseppe 8. Tel: 0782 802641. Open: summer Tue–Sun 10am–1pm & 4.30–7.30pm; winter Tue–Sun 10am–1pm & 4–7pm. Admission charge.

Nuraghe Is Paras: Open: Apr–Oct daily 9.30am–12.30pm & 4.30–7.30pm; Nov–Mar daily 9.30am–12.30pm. Admission charge.

Láconi

Known as 'The Assisi of Sardinia', the town of Láconi was the birthplace of Sant Ignazio, a Capuchin monk who lived from 1701 to 1781 and was deified in 1951. There is a museum to this most

Hiking sign and shrine in the Gennargentu

Apr–Sept daily 9am–1pm & 4–7pm;
Oct–Mar daily 9am–1pm & 4–6pm.
Closed: 1st Mon of the month.
Admission charge.

Mamoiada

The heartland of Gennargentu 'culture', Mamoiada is famed for its incredible carnival rituals that are said to date back to pagan times. If you cannot make it to the island in February or March to see the real thing, then visit the **Museo delle Maschere Mediterranee** (Museum of Mediterranean Masks) to see the masks and costumes and a video presentation of what happens during the big day. The hairy *Mamuthones* are incredibly powerful and it is easy to imagine the effect on villagers in times gone by, when these mystical creatures ushered in good spirits for another year. Carnival costumes from other countries, including Greece and Croatia, are also on show in the small gallery.

Museo delle Maschere Mediterranee: Piazza Europa 15. Tel: 0784 569018; www.museodellemaschere.it. Open: Tue–Sun 9am–1pm & 3–7pm. Admission charge.

famous son, where, among more obvious souvenirs, the finger of the saint is preserved. A statue of a boy on a rearing horse on the outskirts of town relates to a moment in Ignazio's childhood when he was saved from certain death by divine intervention. There is also an interesting **Museo delle Statue Menhir** (Menhir Museum) with a range of these carved standing stones.

On the outskirts of town look out for the remains of Castello Aymerich built in 1051 that sit in the heart of a preserved parkland. The countryside around the town is dotted with other menhirs and is known for its free-roaming Sarcidani horses, a sub-species unique to the island.

Museo delle Statue Menhir: Via Amiscora. Tel: 0782 866216. Open:

Orgosolo

In the north of the region close to Nuoro and Mamoiada, this village sits in some of the most intense rocky landscape in the Gennargentu, and its people have developed a fearsome reputation for banditry. However, in the last few years, the town has been equally renowned for its public murals. First begun as a protest against the social injustices of 20th-century life, they are now an art form.

Osini

The Nuraghic village of **Serbissi** is a complicated set-up, with several tholoi and eight stone houses plus a large natural cave known to have been used to store food. The complex was inhabited between the 18th and 10th centuries BC.

Close by is the **Gola di San Giorgio** (San Giorgio Gully), a narrow rocky valley cut by vertical faults. It is named after San Giorgio, who is said to have prayed for an easier path through the mountains, which, according to the legend, this valley miraculously opened up.

Serbissi: Open: Apr–Oct daily 9.30am–12.30pm & 4.30–7.30pm; Nov–Mar Tue–Sun 9.30am–12.30pm. Admission charge.

Costa Verde

The beaches of the Costa Verde are some of the least visited and most unspoiled on the island and offer an excellent chance to play Robinson Crusoe for a day. The reason for this is its relative isolation, with few access roads and no coastal resorts. Those who make the effort are

Rural landscape of the Gennargentu

rewarded by emerald green waters and golden sands.

The coast is named after the blanket of verdant wild scrubland that hugs the dunes, but it is not a uniform coastline as you will also find sheer cliffs here. **Spiaggia Scivu** in the south is an exceptional stretch of sand, perfect for a long stroll. Further north is **Piscinas**, backed by dunes rising over 30m (98ft). All around you will see evidence that this was a thriving area during the 19th century, with the now abandoned buildings once part of a profitable mining operation.

In the far north, the best beach is at **Torre dei Corsari**, where a decrepit tower watches over the bathers.

The Costa Verde comes to a southern halt at **Capo Pecora**, from where there are long-range views north towards Oristano and south to Buggeru and the distant Isola di San Pietro.

Isola Asinara

Cut off from the Stintino peninsula at the very northwest tip of the island by a narrow channel, Isola Asinara has had a chequered history. A quarantine station opened in the 1860s, and it hosted Sardinia's maximum security detention facility in the 20th century, its relative isolation acting as a deterrent against escape, rather like a Mediterranean-style Alcatraz.

Today, Asinara is a National Park and is named after the population of donkeys that have thrived since being freed from domestic service. They roam

Cows on an isolated beach

free along with families of wild boar. This is excellent walking country with some wild, low landscapes and the occasional abandoned building, either a medieval tower built by the Doria (*see pp96–7*) or one of the old quarantine buildings. The best beach is Cala Sabina, with a crescent of pale sand. During the summer you can hire bikes. However, you will need to take a picnic with you because, as yet, there are no refreshment kiosks or cafés on the island.

You can reach the island from Stintino (see p106) or from Porto Torres (see pp103–4) in high season.

Pattada and environs

A centre of knife production, the village has several shops where you can buy good examples. The area around Pattada is largely unexplored.

Ozieri to the west is the region's largest town, once the heartland of the Ozieri peoples who inhabited Sardinia in ancient times. The town's **Museo Archeologico** (Archaeological Museum) displays finds excavated from a cave site, Grotta di San Michele, close to the town, which is also open to the public. The **Cattedrale dell'Immacolata**, with its Gothic heart contained in ornate neoclassical wrappings, is worth a look.

South of Pattada, among a cluster of hills, are the several natural thermal springs that form low-key resorts offering wellness treatments. **Benetutti** (*see p163*) and **Terme di San Saturnino** both have up-to-date facilities.
Museo Archeologico: Piazza San Francesco. Tel: 079 787638. Open: Tue–Sun 9am–1pm & 4–7.30pm. Admission charge; combined fee with Grotta di San Michele, which shares the same hours.

Winding mountain roads

Getting away from it all

Drive: The eastern Gennargentu

Head throughout the heartland of rural Sardinia on this day-long journey, where you will come face to face with the forces of pagan power and marvel at nature's beauty, both along the coast and inland.

Time: 8 hours.

Distance: 330km (205 miles).

Start the day at Nuoro.

1 Nuoro

Spend the first part of the day exploring the attractions of Nuoro (*see pp118–20*).

Leave Nuoro from the northeast on the SS129 signposted Orosei. The road travels down a steep valley with views out across the countryside through Galtelli until after 40km (25 miles) you reach Orosei.

2 Orosei

This tiny enclave of small cottages has several churches set around the cobbled square. To the west are some excellent beaches, but it is too early in the trip to take a break.

Leave Orosei from the south following signs to Dorgali. The road leads past some of the island's biggest and most active quarries and you will probably pass several large lorries carrying huge cubes of just-cut stone. Take care here. After 21km (13 miles) you will reach Dorgali.

3 Dorgali

The main street in Dorgali snakes up and around the hillside. Along the way there are lots of shops selling excellent handicrafts and a couple of good outdoor pursuit companies offering guided hikes or adventure sports in the region.

Follow the main route (SS125) south, signposted Tortoli and Arbatax. As the road begins to climb, you will see a sign for the beach at Cala Gonone, reached via a tunnel through Monte Tului. As you head south, you will drive through some fine mountainscapes with views across the peaks to the west. You will be tempted to stop at more than one view point en route. After 48km (30 miles) you will reach Baunei.

4 Baunei

Baunei clings limpet-like to its easterly-facing hillside. Above the town is Il Golgo, a 270m (886ft) hole in the mountain that is a favourite location for free-climbers and abseilers. *Continue south for another 16km (10 miles) until you reach the left turn for Arbatax.*

The landscape around Nuoro

5 Arbatax

Arbatax has a small selection of cafés and restaurants and it will be a while before you get another chance for a coffee. Hunt out the 'red rocks' just south of the pleasure port (drive right to the end of the road through town). *Leave Arbatax, then follow the SS198 in the direction of Nuoro. After 21km (13 miles) the road splits. You will follow signs for Gairo (straight ahead as the crow flies), heading up a verdant valley through the town of Seui. The route travels through excellent peaks and valleys until 77km (48 miles) from Tortoli you take a right turn to Seulo and Tonara.*

6 Seulo and Tonara

This route is the heartland of the Barbagia, a country road through the heights of Sardinia with oak forests and grazing land and majestic views around every corner.
Continue to Tonara, then take a left turn out of the village to pick up the SS128 to Fonni. Travel through Tiana and Ovodda and when you reach Fonni (winter ski 'resort') take the route for Nuoro, the SS389 to Mamoiada.

7 Mamoiada

Mamoiada is famed for the Museum of Masks and it is the place to find out about the region's carnival traditions.
From Mamoiada continue on the SS389 and after 18km (11 miles) you will be back in Nuoro.

Shopping

Souvenir hunters will have a great time on Sardinia. The island nurtures traditional industries as an important part of its living culture and there are good numbers of artisans working in many arts and crafts, producing high-quality handmade goods. There is bound to be something for you to pack in your suitcase, either to adorn your body or to adorn your home.

Basket-weaving

Hand weaving of grasses – rushes, reeds, lentisk and straw – has a long history, including woven grass boats on the marshes around Oristano, though modern items are both decorative and practical. Larger items are created by a wicker technique, whereas smaller examples involve long 'ropes' of natural grass being wound into shape and held together by grass 'twine'. Castelsardo is one centre for this craft and you will see ladies sitting in their doorways weaving mats, small jars or decorative plaques. The other important modern centre is San Vero Milis in Sinnai.

Ceramics

The ample raw materials for ceramics meant a thriving industry from man's earliest history on the island. Although there were two ceramics schools established on Sardinia in the 1920s, what the artisans excel in is decorative but practical objects such as jars, jugs and bowls. Patterns often hark back to the Nuraghic or Roman styles, or themes come from the countryside.

Foodstuffs

You can stock your larder with high-quality produce after a trip to Sardinia. The pecorino cheese can be used in the same way as Parmesan and makes very tasty cheese on toast! Dried meats such as salami and hams make a delicious charcuterie plate, or look for herb-scented honey or excellent olive oil – very fragrant and great on salads. Although expensive by UK supermarket prices, the tinned tuna is excellent quality as only the best cuts are preserved in good olive oil. This smorgasbord can all be washed down with some surprisingly good wines (*see pp172–3*). Take some of these back and you can wow your friends with the new discovery at your next dinner party.

Jewellery

Sardinian jewellery was one of the most sought-after luxury items of the medieval world. The gold- and silversmiths were highly skilled and produced extremely intricate work. Today, though much of the jewellery is mass-produced, you can still find artisans working by hand, and prices are not outrageous.

Jewellery has been excavated from ancient burial sites and styles are now copied for the modern market, but the island is most famed for its filigree, a technique where fine strands of precious metal are bent and woven into brooches, rings or pendants to hang on necklaces.

Visit any of the traditional festivals and you will see women adorned with jewellery, worn on traditional costumes like war medals on a uniform. Jewellery was a way of safeguarding a family's wealth, but it would be paraded on special occasions as clasps on waistcoats or headdresses.

Look out also for the 'maninfide' ring (carved hands clasped), which a man gave to a woman upon betrothal. In return he would receive a good-quality knife (*see pp150–51*).

Amulets of all kinds were produced to ward off evil spirits but are now just

Basketware from Castelsardo depicts a fine indigenous skill

decorative items. Mother-of-pearl was often used, while obsidian jewellery was put in a baby's cradle to protect him or her while sleeping.

Sardinia is also famed for its coral jewellery. This now highly controlled industry takes its beautiful pink raw material from the seabed and then has it carved or set in silver and gold. However, bear in mind that the animals have been hugely overharvested over the years and red coral can now be found only in the deeper parts of the Mediterranean (*see www.toopreciousotowear.org*).

Weaving

Not so long ago every household on the island had a loom, and weaving was part of everyday life for the women who would make blankets, rugs and other household items from natural materials such as wool and linen. Today, weaving is still a strong cottage industry, with production in about forty villages. There are over a hundred traditional patterns and twenty *mustras* or central themes, including stylised people, animals and floral motifs. Colours have always been produced from hues from natural sources – for example, soils, plants and animal matter.

There are several weaving techniques, including a *stuoia*, or smooth weave, and a *pibiones*, where the yarn is twisted to create a raised 'grain' of yarn (*pibiones* means grains) that creates an ornate raised pattern on the surface of the material.

Wooden carved objects

Country life was simple, but every household has three or four good pieces of wooden furniture that were passed down through the generations, including a trousseau blanket box given to every young girl, where she collected items for her married life.

Wood was in ready supply, mainly walnut and juniper, and the traditions of woodcarving are as strong as ever, especially in the Barbagia region. You can have bespoke items made and shipped home.

The pagan carnival masks (*see pp22 & 28*) also make a unique souvenir. Handmade pieces are exquisite but expensive, though there are some mass-produced items around.

All kinds of cheeses, with special daily offers

Traditional Sardinian ceramics

WHERE TO SHOP

The streets of old Cágliari, Alghero and Castelsardo are the best places to browse, but you will find craft shops in all tourist resorts. Note that shopping opportunities will be fewer in most resorts between mid-September and early May.

Look out also for colourful markets that take place at least once weekly in major towns. This is where you can buy foodstuffs and handicrafts, though not the best handmade examples, at the best prices. Here are a few good purveyors from around the island:

EAST
Dorgali
Esseffe (Laborato Orafo di Francesco Serra)
Francesco Serra produces hand-worked filigree and other jewellery at his workshop.
Corso Umberto 72. Tel: 0784 96780.

Orosei
Floral Design
A pretty range of *objets d'art* in this craft shop cum florists.
Piazza del Popolo 1. Tel: 0784 89702.

Ulassai
SuMarmuri
Weaving workshop producing top-quality rugs, throws and other textiles.
Via Funtana Serì. Tel: 0782 79706.

NORTHWEST
Alghero
Aradena
Top-of-the-range traditional knives, rugs, ceramics, jewellery and many other goods.
Via Gioberti 24/28. Tel: 079 9735058.

Coralli di Sardegna
Excellent range of coral jewellery and objects in all price ranges.
Via Carlo Alberto 67.
Tel: 079 980093;
www.corallidisardegna.it

Castelsardo
Il Castellano
Quality island foodstuffs and high-quality knives.
Via Mazzini 5. Tel: 079 470176.

WEST
Oristano
I Fenicotteri (di Giuseppe Pippia)
A good shop for a whole range of island crafts, traditional and modern.
Corso Umberto 50. Tel: 0783 78077.

Sardinian knives

The most famous artisan craft on Sardinia is knife-making. Though not your run-of-the-mill souvenir, knives have been an important tool throughout the island's history, whether for shepherds out in the countryside, fishermen at sea or miners working underground.

Knives had to be strong and last a long time, so quality was paramount. Over time this developed into a highly respected and high-skilled cottage industry, though, as with many things on Sardinia, the regional differences and rivalries across the island have seen the development of a number of varying styles.

Today, the knife industry worldwide is dominated by mass production, but here you can still find a population of skilled artisans making individual knives by hand (expensive) or small cottage workshops using a semi-automated approach with a craftsman's finish (less expensive).

The Arburesa knife

The Arburesa knife comes from Arbus in southwestern Sardinia and it is preferred by hunters and those skinning animals because it is a wide-bladed knife and both strong and flexible.

An Arburesa knife made by Paolo Pusceddu holds the official world record for the largest 'pocket knife', with a length of 3.65m (almost 12ft), which you can see at the Knife Museum in Arbus. Some Arburesa knives are machine-made.

The Pattadesa

The Pattadesa knife was originally produced in Pattada in northern Sardinia and is the most famous of Sardinian knives. The blade folds back into the body, making it compact and safer to carry. The knife was originally the tool of choice for shepherds, who on many occasions needed to defend themselves and their flocks. The Pattadesa was made in different weights and sizes and originally used metal from old bayonets for the blades. The ferrule was decorated. The Pattadesa knife should be artisan-made as Sardinians don't recognise any industrial production.

The Guspinesa

The Guspinesa knife was traditionally made in Guspini in southwestern Sardinia and it is called a miner's knife, mainly used to cut and smear but not to stab (though they could still be used as a weapon). This knife is used as a cutting-blade rather than having a point at the end.

The Guspinesa became famous during World War I, when it was carried by the Brigata Sassari and used in hand-to-hand combat.

How knives are made

The horn is carefully chosen, then softened by heat and shaped over a vice. The steel is heated to a temperature of around 900°C (1,650°F) and the understanding of temperature is very important for the strength of the finished knife. Two elements need to be completed: the steel core between the horn, and the blade. Steel and brass pins are used to bring the knife together. The handle and blade are polished and the cutting blade is sharpened.

Master craftsmen

Paolo Pusceddu is undoubtedly the leading light among today's craftsmen. His knives are highly sought after and at his workshop at Arbus he has opened an excellent museum to the art.

Antonio Cau, from San Gavino, is one of a new generation of knife-makers. In his mid-20s, he learned at the hands of master Silvano Usai from Sinnai. He runs a workshop in Guspini, making Pattadesa and Guspinesa knives.

This formidable display of knives represents a unique Sardinian craft, respected the world over. Each knife is a speciality and made by skilful hands

Entertainment

With so many of the world's rich and famous living or holidaying on Sardinia, its playgrounds unsurprisingly offer a rich array of choices. While nature's playing fields are there in abundance, so are the ones created by man. From discos and special clubs to theatres, where the music and drama season attracts both local and visiting lovers of these arts, you will never be bored or tired of the same thing.

CLUBS AND DISCOS

During the high season, the resorts across the island can match anywhere in the Mediterranean for their clubs and discos. There are some excellent open-air venues, where you can dance till dawn and many of the most upmarket operations combine dining, piano bar and club in one complex. However, as soon as the season ends in mid-September, everything closes down and you will need to head to the major towns for any night action. Porto Cervo and greater Costa Smeralda is where the well heeled head. Cágliari has the best year-round scene, where the locals and the large student crowds head at the weekend.

Alghero
Mique de Mirall
A chilled-out disco with snakeskin stools, flamingo-orange walls and well-stocked bar.
Piazza Manno 14. Tel: 3475 844475. Open: Mon–Sat 5pm–2am.

Cágliari
Go Fish
Cágliari's most raucous gay and drag club/disco welcomes all adult clients.
Via Venturi 12/14. Tel: 070 4529086; www.go-fish.it
New Open Gate
With guest DJs and a more inventive repertoire, New Open Gate is the place to escape the humdrum dance venues.
Via Venturi 18. Tel: 070 496969.
Spazio Newton
It has been on the scene for a while and is as popular as ever.
Via Newton II. Tel: 070 496969; www.spazionewton.com

Costa Smeralda
Billionaire Disco
Home of the rich, famous and blue-blooded, so you will have to fit the entry requirements to get in; at least dress to the nines and look as if you should own the place.

Golfo Pevero, Porto Cervo.
Tel: 0789 94192.

Ritual Discoteca

This huge open-air venue is built
into the hillside like an old stone
village and blended into the
surrounding rock landscape.
La Crucitta, Baia Sardinia.
Tel: 0789 99032;
www.ritual.it

Sopravento

Like Billionaire Disco, another upmarket
venue, with a strict entry code.
Loc Abbiadori, Porto Cervo.
Tel: 0789 94717.

Sottovento

Completing the trio of where
to be seen for the Costa Smeralda
jet-set.
Loc Abbiadori, Porto Cervo.
Tel: 0789 92443.

Pula
Corte Noa

Open-air disco and *ristorante* that
draws a crowd from Cágliari on
summer weekends.
SS195 km 32.5, Santa Maria di Pula.

Quartu Sant'Elena
FBI Club

Popular American-style dance club on
Saturdays and Sundays, combined with
the Al Capone pizzeria.
Brigata Sassari 68. Tel: 070 882332;
www.fbiclub.it

San Teodoro
La Luna Disco Glam Club

This truly lives up to its name, with a
very upmarket interior – dress for it.
Loc Stirritoggiu. Tel: 338 9789776;
www.lalunadisco.com

The cocktail bar at Mique de Mirall nightclub in Alghero

FESTIVALS

The major festivals have already been mentioned in the Festivals and events section (*see pp28–9*), but traditional festivities are such an important element of the entertainment scene that some more are added here.

Food festivals

Many Sardinian festivals turn into a food-fest with lots of traditional dishes, but there is a full calendar of festivals relating specifically to food, normally around a particular harvest, to whet your appetite and enjoy.

End May and early June
Tuna Festival Carloforte
(Carbonia-Iglesias province)
June
Peach Festival
San Sparate (Cágliari province).
Tundimenta Seulesa
Sheep-shearing festival with the traditional foods associated with the shepherd's lifestyle.
Seulo (Nuoro province).
July
Culurgione Festival
Tortolì (Ogliastra province).
Fish Festival
Santa Teresa Gallura (Olbia-Tempio province).
August
Fish Festival
Castelsardo (Sassari province).
Vermentino Wine Festival
Monti (Olbia-Tempio province).
Wild Boar Festival
Dómus de Maria (Cágliari province).
Wine Festival
Famed for its Cannonau wine.
Jerzu (Ogliastra province).
November
Novello d'Oro
Ride from Cágliari to Arzana on the Little Green Train to taste the new wines plus traditional dishes.
Vini Novelli
New wines are released.
Milis (Oristano province).

Music festivals

Some of the smallest island communities are renowned for their music festivals and it is a wonderful way to while away a summer evening.

Classical
Estate Musicale Internazionale di Alghero
A series of classical music concerts held in the cloisters of the Chiesa di San Francesco in July and August.

Jazz
Ai Confini tra Sardegna e Jazz
A combination of traditional music and exploratory jazz in this well-established festival at the end of August.
Sant'Anna Arresi (Carbonia-Iglesias province). Tel: 0781 996861; www.santannarresijazz.it
Cala Gonone Jazz
International jazz performances at the end of July and during the first few days of August.

Cala Gonone (Nuoro province).
Tel: 0784 232539.

Time in Jazz

Yet more trad and improv in another part of the island, this time in mid-August.
Berchidda (Olbia-Tempio province).
Tel: 079 703007; www.timeinjazz.it

Blues

Narcao Blues

Three days of live concerts with local and international bands and musicians, mid- to late July.
Narcao (Carbonia-Iglesias province).
Tel: 0781 959489; www.narcaoblues.it

CLASSICAL PERFORMANCES

Sardinia is part of the country that gave us opera, so it is not surprising that it has a vibrant season of arts performances. Opera and ballet are internationally understood genres, but the theatre will be a bit pointless if you don't understand Italian.

Cágliari

The Fundacio Teatro Lirico di Cágliari organises a year-round programme of events. The opera and ballet season runs from October to June with performances at Cágliari Opera House (Via Sant'Alenixedda). In summer the performances move outdoors to the Cágliari Roman amphitheatre, where there is a summer festival.
Ticket office for both venues is Via Sant'Alenixedda; tel: 070 4082230; www.teatroliricodicagliari.it.

Open: Wed–Fri 10am–2pm & 6–8pm; Sat 10am–2pm.

There are ten other theatres in the capital along with the Auditorium Comunale (via Dettori; tel: 070 201691).

Around the island

All the major towns on Sardinia have theatre houses with active theatre groups. Sassari has three venues, the 19th-century Teatro Civico (*Corso Vittorio Emanuele, tel: 079 232182*), the Teatro Verdi (*Via Politeama, tel: 079 239479*) and the Teatro Il Ferroviario (*Corso Vico 14, tel: 079 2633049*), which offers more modern and improvised performances.

In Alghero, the season revolves around the Teatro Civico in Alghero (*Piazza del Teatro, tel: 079 997880*). In Tempio Pausania, the Teatro del Carmine (*Piazza del Carmine, tel: 079 635144*) offers a full programme of plays and concerts from October to May, plus the summer Festival d'Estate concerts.

Performance posters offer a wide choice of venues where you can spend an evening

Children

Though there are few activities or attractions specifically designed for children, Sardinia certainly has plenty to offer but will appeal especially to active older children (8+) who love being outdoors. You will find a warm welcome at restaurants around the island, where family meals are often a long and boisterous affair, and no child ever turned their nose up at pizza or spaghetti, so the food is never any problem.

Beach activities

Sardinian beaches are so numerous that you can easily combine a trip to an ancient site or a morning of urban sightseeing with a couple of hours at the beach.

The waters are some of the cleanest in Europe, crystal clear and usually calm in summer: perfect for swimming and snorkelling. On top of the water try your hand at windsurfing, kayaking and waterskiing; they are guaranteed to tire out even the most energetic child.

Boat trips

Children love getting out on to the water, and the choice of day trips from almost anywhere on the coast is great for filling a day or two. Full-day organised trips always offer lunch and usually time for swimming too. For further details on boat trips on offer, *see pp96, 112 & 114.*

For something more unusual try heading under the water in a mini submarine to get a closer look at the marine life.

Dotto trains

There are 'dotto train' tours of Cágliari, Alghero and other resorts and towns during the summer season. A good way to see the attractions but an even better way to ensure that little legs don't get over-tired.

The safe beaches are ideal for family holidays

Festivals

The full diary of summer festivals always offers something for children, be it parades with traditional costumes, Sardinian song and dance, religious processions or old-fashioned funfairs. The major festivals and events for the whole island are listed on pages 28–9, but this is only the tip of the iceberg and you will find that there are numerous other smaller fairs in each region for you to enjoy.

Consult your local tourist office when you get to Sardinia to find out what is going on.

Horse riding

Trekking is popular and most stables cater to all levels of ability. Treks can last from a couple of hours to a whole day (with lunch) and offer a slower-paced way to see a bit of the Sardinian countryside.

Lessons are also usually available, but not all instructors speak English.

Ice cream

Ice cream (*gelato*) is an institution in Italy, so if all else fails head to the nearest ice-cream shop. The delicious flavours soothe even the most fevered brow, for both adults and children!

Sports and outdoor pursuits

The mountain biking and cycling and hiking/rambling possibilities are seemingly endless. For children with cycling proficiency the island makes a perfect place for exploration, with landscapes like the marshlands north of Oristano or the bays north of Alghero being flat and easy to get around. Cycle hire is easy and cheap.

Water parks

With such wonderful clean water supplied by nature, it is not surprising that water parks are still thin on the ground. But if your children prefer fresh water to salt water there is Bluefan just north of Pula in the south and Aquadream water park at Baia Sardinia just north of the Costa Smeralda. Both open June–mid-September only.

An ice-cream shop in Alghero

Sport and leisure

Whatever your interests, Sardinia will probably be able to provide the facilities. Watersports naturally feature prominently and, on land, the island offers wonderful terrain for walking and horse riding, with opportunities in the Barbagia region for skiing, caving and canyoning. To recover from your exertions, sample one of the island's spas.

Spectator sports
Football
Sardinia has a top-flight club, Cágliari, or the Rosoblu, which did the unthinkable in 1970 and won Lo Scudetto, the then version of the League Championship. It has been a rather mixed picture since then. They dropped as far as Serie C in 1987 but are back in Serie A, though fighting for survival in the lower half of the division.

Tickets are not easy to come by, but the season runs from September to May.

Stadium: Viale la Playa, Cágliari. Tel: 070 604201.

Sardinian wrestling
Now very much a minority sport, Sardinian wrestling, or S'Istrumpa, is still practised in its heartland, the wild Barbagia.

The contests started among the shepherds and was a sort of social sparring to establish social bonds, and to distinguish the strong from the weak in a society where strength was highly respected.

S'Istrumpa style has the two combatants standing face to face with hands clasped behind each other's backs, what is called a 'back hold' in the sport. From this stance each must try to push the other on to his back while maintaining the hand hold.

The sport was almost lost in the years after World War II but is now being taught to a new generation of Sardinian youth, and a federation, affiliated to the International Federation of Celtic Wrestling, has been formed. Contact the tourist office in Nuoro for details of competitions held in the region. The sport was traditionally practised at Bargabia weddings and can still sometimes be seen if you are lucky enough to get an invite.

Motorsport
Since 2004, Sardinia has played host to the Italian round of the World Rally

Championship with three days of gruelling competition on the roads around the Costa Smeralda at the end of April or in early May.

For more details see the WRC website *www.wrc.com*.

The same region also hosts its own Rally Costa Smeralda later in the year, usually in early December. This is another FIA-organised event with a longer island pedigree. For more details see the FIA website *www.fia.com*

Regattas

Porto Cervo is at the forefront of the competitive sailing world, one of the few select ports in this part of the Mediterranean that are on the sailing circuit. When competitions take place the whole resort is buzzing and, although it is not the easiest sport to watch for spectators, the atmosphere is palpable.

Main events include:

April –	Vela and Golf Regatta
May –	Capri Sailing Clinic and the Coppa Europa
June –	The Grand Soleil Cup
July –	The Jeep Challenge
September –	Rolex Settimana delle Bocche and Rolex Maxi Yachts

Contact Yacht Club Costa Smeralda (Via della Marina, Porto Cervo. Tel: 0789 902200; www.yccs.it) for details of exact dates.

Participation sports

It is difficult to imagine better conditions for sports, with warm weather from April to October and long sunny days, and unspoiled coastal and countryside

Yachting is ever popular here

landscapes to enjoy. Sardinia is a great location for many extreme sports, but you will find many mainstream activities too.

Canyoning

Sardinia was one of the first places to popularise canyoning. This adrenalin sport has you heading down watercourses by almost any means possible with dinghies, ropes or by diving down water chutes. The Barbagia region has lots of canyoning options. Barbagia No Limits (*see Caving*) offers guided tours.

Spectacular views from the saddle in the Gennargentu

Caving

There is a maze of cave systems and caverns cutting through Sardinian rock and, for those with an adventurous spirit and average fitness, companies can organise guided discovery tours. Barbagia No Limits is based in this wild and dramatic part of the island and heads into the caves of Barbagia and Ogliastra.
Barbagia No Limits: Via Cágliari 85, Gavoi. Tel: 0784 529016; www.barbagianolimits.it

Diving

Although sea life is not as colourful and varied as in the Caribbean, Sardinia has many advantages over other destinations in the Mediterranean, with excellent water quality and a varied coast. There are lots of dive companies that will offer training for beginners and equipment rental and support to qualified divers, but be aware that not all companies have English-speaking staff.
Here are some dive centres to contact:
Adventure & Diving: Porto Conte Marina Tel: 079 942205; www.algherovacaze.com/diving
Aqua Diving Centre: Puntaldia, San Teodoro. Tel: 348 5112333; www.diving.it
Asinara Diving Center: Poto dell'Ancora, Stintino. Tel: 079 527000; www.asinaradivingcenter.com
Centro Subacqueo Yacht Club Cágliari: Porticciolo di Marina, Piccola Yacht Club, Poetta. Tel: 070 370350.
Isla Diving: Corso Battelieri 21, Carloforte. Tel: 0781 855634; www.isladiving.it

Golf

Sardinia is taking its fair share of the golf market, and its fine autumn and spring weather makes it a great out-of-season location for a little putting practice.

Golf Club Puntaldia: Part of a nicely planned hotel resort.

Due Lune Resort and Golf, San Teodoro. Tel: 0784 864470.

Is Arenas Golf and Country Club: Open all year, this country club can also handle organising your complete holiday package if you need to book hotels, car hire, etc.

Loc Pineta Is Arenas, Narbolia. Tel: 0783 52036; www.isarenas.it

Is Molas: Part of a luxury resort hotel on the coast south of the capital.

Santa Maria di Pula. Tel: 070 9241006; www.ismolas.it

Il Pevero: This Robert Trent Jones designed course serves the 'monied' coast. It is open year round.

Loc Cala di Volpe, Costa Smeralda. Tel: 0789 958000; www.golfclubpevero.com

Hiking and walking

Sardinia is a walking and trekking destination, be it along the coast or in the heart of the hilly Barbagia and Gennargentu, where you can enjoy the rural life that still thrives. If you would liked guided hikes contact Barbagia No Limits (*see Caving*), who can design routes and accompany your trip.

Horse riding

Sardinians still have a close affinity with horses, especially in the countryside. For visitors, there is so much more to see from the back of a horse, and the one-horsepower four-leg mode of travel is much better over rough country tracks than a car. It is somehow much easier to connect with your surroundings, be they sea-spray or fragrant wild herbs. There are plenty of horses for hire in Sardinia and if you are already experienced that is great. Riding lessons are also easy to find, but not necessarily in English.

Specialists and beginners can safely kayak in the calm protected bays of Sardinia

For further information on riding schools on the island contact:
Istituto Incremento Ippico della Sardegna:
Piazza Borgia 4, Ozieri. Tel: 079 787852; www.sardegnacavalli.it (Italian only).

Forty riding centres have organised a website and guide: *Guide Equestri Ambienti:*
Oasi di Sale Porcus, San Vero Milis. Tel: 0783 528100; www.sitogea.net (Italian only).

For lessons and trekking in the north of the island: *Centro Ippico Santa Teresa Gallura:*
La Testa, Santa Teresa Gallura. Tel: 340 8508293 (mobile number); www.sardinienreiter.de (information also in English).

Sailing (*see pp164–5*)

Skiing

There is only a fledgling ski industry on the island, but the runs at Fonni (*see map, p144*) might make an enjoyable afternoon on the snow with runs down nearby Bruncu Spina. The season runs roughly from December to April depending on snow conditions.

Surfing

Sardinia has been called the 'Hawaii of the Mediterranean' and is certainly one of the prime European locations for its waves, the quality of its water and the number of surfing spots available in totally awesome landscapes. Most surf beaches are pretty empty on out-of-season weekdays, but weekends bring young sportsmen from the city to show off their moves.

Several beaches around Cágliari have a good reputation, including Su Poettu, Porto Pino and Marina di Capitano at the end of Poetto Beach close to the capital. Further afield at Chia there is usually good water. Close to Oristano head north to San Giovanni di Sinis or Capo Mannu, or, in the northwest, east of Porto Torres or around Stintino.

Surfboards are not easy to hire, so you would do better to bring your own.

Watersports

All the major resorts have watersports and there are concessions on the beach from June to mid-September.

Jet-skiing is great for speed merchants while sea kayaking allows you to explore the long coastline with its inlets and quiet coves at a more relaxing pace and under your own steam.

Windsurfing

Sardinia's many and varied beaches face in all directions, and on almost any given day somewhere on the island will have perfect conditions for windsurfing. Aficionados flock to the island, and if you are a beginner it is a great place to learn.

Beaches at all the major resorts have windsurf boards to hire during high season, but for remote spots you will need your own equipment.

Porto Pollo or Porto Puddu close to Palau is a renowned spot that is said to be the best on the island because of its almost perfect wind conditions, though this can be taxing for novices. Chia is enjoyed by windsurfers and surfers but offers easier waters. Close to the capital try Poetto beach or Villasimius on the southeast coast.

Spas and wellbeing

Sardinia offers some excellent opportunities for true relaxation and pampering, with a number of hotels offering spa and other wellness treatments.

Benetutti Terme in central Sardinia takes advantage of a natural source of mineral and radioactive water (beneficial, not dangerous!) and there are several hotels in the town.

Aurora Terme (*Benetutti Terme. Tel: 079 796871*) is a three-star hotel with a range of skin treatment and thalassotherapy while the S'Astore Hotel (*Benetutti Terme. Tel: 079 796620*) is a four-star establishment offering similar spa treatments.

Terme del Porto (*Porto Touristico, Santa Teresa Gallura. Tel: 0789 741078; www.termedelporto.com*) is open year round; it has a day spa and offers fitness and posture, physical therapy, osteopathy, hammam (Turkish steam bath), sauna and massage.

The large five-star complex of Forte Village (*Santa Maria di Pula, on a peninsula south of Pula. Tel: 070 921516; www.fortevillage.com*) has the best facilities on the island and the only full-service day spa on Sardinia.

Some waves may catch you unawares

Yachting

The magnificent coastline and offshore islands, combined with crystal-clear summer seas, make Sardinia a prime sailing destination, but it is almost unknown outside Italy and just waiting to be discovered by the rest of the world. Some of the island's most unspoiled bays can only be reached by boat or on foot, and there are few better feelings in the world than dropping anchor at your own private cove, surrounded by azure waters with a hint of golden sand, where the only sound you can hear is the lapping of the waves.

Marinas

Marinas on Sardinia vary in size and in their facilities. The most basic offer berths and fresh water, while the most modern will have electrical hook-ups for boats, shower facilities

Luxury yachts lined up at Porto Cervo

and even accommodation. Ports are well organised for the yachting crowd. The most romantic are those where you can disembark and sit on the quayside enjoying an aperitif or dinner at a restaurant overlooking the yachts.

Popular ports of call

The upmarket ports of the Costa Smeralda, Porto Cervo and Porto Rotondo, are without doubt the prime spots on the island if you want to be seen among European royalty and the mega-rich; they will even throw in a celebrity or two. However, you will have to drop anchor among some of the most expensive boats on the Mediterranean and their posse of well-groomed and uniformed staff.

Not all ports of call require that you take out a mortgage before mooring up. Better to head to Palau or the Maddalena Islands close to the Costa Smeralda, Alghero, Sant'Antioco or Carloforte, where the attitude is more relaxed and the prices more in keeping with the rest of Sardinia.

Getting organised

If you have a day skipper's certificate, you will be allowed to take a boat yourself (a bareboat). With no certificate you will need to hire a captain to take you around. Better still, hire a fully equipped boat with a cook and cleaner so that you have got nothing to worry about but how to relax and build your tan.

'Just Sardinia' is an island travel specialist that offers both staffed and bareboat yachting. Contact them at:
Royalties House
4 Fairfield Close
Christchurch
Dorset
BH23 1QZ
Tel: 01202 484848;
www.justsardinia.co.uk

The Day Skipper Certificate
This card is like the basic driving licence for cars and allows 'the skipper' to be responsible for the safety of his/her boat and crew for day sailing (in daylight only), in local waters (not too far from the shore, not out in the open ocean), and requiring only basic navigational skills, in moderate wind and sea conditions. Normally, study for the

A yacht sailing on the clear waters

certificate takes five days or three weekends, with a written test at the end.

In the UK the Royal Yachting Association is the leading body for sailing training and information relating to developments. Contact them at:
RYA House
Ensign Way
Hamble
Southampton
SO31 4YA
Tel: 0845 345 0400 or 023 8060 4100; www.rya.org.uk

SOMETHING WITH MORE OOMPH

If sailing is not for you, perhaps a trip along the coastline in a powerboat is more your style. IBS, Porto Rotondo, Olbia, *tel: 0789 380048; www.ibsgroup.it* has all the toys you might want to play with.

Birdwatching

Sardinia is an excellent birdwatching location. The ever-changing landscape provides a varied habitat, from the cultivated farmland, grazing meadows and rugged hills of the interior, which are perfect for Falconiformes and Accipitriformes (birds of prey to the lay person) and for Galliformes (game birds), to the miles of cliffs, sandy bays and hectares of wetland that attract Pelicaniformes (sea birds) and Chadariformes (waders and shore birds). The island is like Grand Central Station in the spring and autumn when dozens of species pit-stop during migratory journeys north or south.

Birdwatching spots

There are wetlands all around the island that form an important habitat for a good range of native and migratory species. The Stagno di Cabras and Golfa della Salines around Oristano are the largest on the island, complemented by extensive wetlands further south around Cágliari, particularly just inland of the Poetta beaches. Other wetland habitats can be found around Cannigione in the northeast just north of the Costa Smeralda and at Stagno di San Teodoro south of Olbia. All these areas are important rest stops for the flocks of migrating flamingoes that draw birdwatchers from around the world.

What you can see
Coasts

In coastal areas you will find sandpipers, Kentish plovers, shovellers, pochards, cormorants and moorhens on the ground and yellow-legged and slender-billed gulls in the skies. Rarer visitors include shearwaters and Audouin's gull.

Marshland

Grebe, egrets and herons love water, salt or fresh, along with numerous species of duck, complemented by Sardinian warblers and bee eaters.

Cliffs

Sea birds love breeding on the cliff tops, but they have competition from

A griffon vulture soars overhead

Flamingoes at Stagno di San Teodoro

lots of other species, including alpine and pallid swifts, warblers, blue rock thrushes, red-rumped swallow and a few Barbary partridge. A couple of good sites are the cliffs close to San Pietro in the southwest and at Capo Caccia west of Alghero.

Countryside and woodland

Inland look out for the great spotted woodpecker, hoopoe, stonechat, firecrest, citril finch, cirl bunting and the skylark.

Birds of prey

Sardinia has an amazing range of raptors in all sizes, starting with the kestrel, which is common all across the island. The Eleonora's falcons that breed close to San Pietro are summer visitors, along with the smaller, and rarer, hobby. Larger examples are peregrine falcons and buzzards, while ospreys swoop and glide across open water at Lago di Cabras.

You won't need to hunt out the population of griffon vultures nesting in the hills between Alghero and Bosa as these huge birds (the largest found on Sardinia at 105cm/3ft 5in tall) are likely to be thermalling any time the skies are clear. And the action does not stop by night because Scops, little, tawny and barn owls are all common and very active.

Useful organisations

The Royal Society for the Protection of Birds (RSPB), The Lodge, Potton Road, Sandy, Beds, SG19 2DL; *tel: 01767 680551; www.rspb.org.uk* provides information and activities for birdwatchers with affiliations to international organisations.
The website *www.birdingpal.org* puts avid birdwatchers around the world in touch with one another, while *www.birdtours.co.uk* has information on holidays and reports from fellow birders about their adventures and 'twitching' successes.

Food and drink

The Italian staples of pizza and pasta are certainly here to stay, but, like many regions of Italy, Sardinia has a whole range of specialist dishes that take into account local agriculture and weather patterns, with a base of exceptional olive oil, succulent fresh fruits and vegetables, and wild herbs.

As Sardinia is surrounded by water, it is not surprising that you will find excellent seafood in all the coastal towns. However, the basics of Sardinian cuisine are about the land, not the sea, because the Sardinians are a pastoral people.

Suckling pig (*porcetto* or *porceddu*) is a speciality of the island; you will see lots of sows and piglets grubbing around the place. *Capretto* (kid goat) and *agnello* (lamb) are also roasted in the same way.

Game is often on the menu, the prime examples being rabbit, partridge and wild boar.

Sardinians love offal, which is often cooked in rich sauces and served as a stew or barbecued over coals.

Although it isn't to everyone's taste, you will find horse and donkey meat on the 'steak' list.

Dessert

An extra-sweet tooth is required for *sebeas*, pastry pockets filled with ricotta cheese and coated in honey, or try *mustazzolus*, a cinnamon bread-cake that is a speciality of the Oristano district. With a glass of sweet Vernaccia (*see p173*) you will normally be served with *gueffus*, almond biscuits for dipping.

How to eat

Italians worship food and do not see meals as something that needs to be crammed in between other activities. Traditionally, Sardinians have tended to eat fewer courses than the four courses favoured by mainland Italians, generally

PASTA PARCELS

Of course you will find pasta all over Italy, but Sardinian specialities include *culurgiones*, small pasta pockets with a variety of fillings. *Gnocchetti sardi* are thick shell-shaped pasta, officially called *mallodoreddus*.

You are not likely to find Bolognese sauce on Sardinian menus. You can order the spaghetti that everyone knows and loves by looking for *ragu*, which is an almost identical rich meat and tomato sauce.

concentrating on a hearty main course accompanied by their delicious fresh bread. However, Sardinia's varied range of dried meats and salamis are often served as antipasti, and, sliced thinly, they make an excellent accompaniment to early evening drinks.

Bread (*pane*) is more than an optional item on Sardinia. The island has numerous speciality items, such as crusty flat unleavened sheets called *pane carasau*, *spianata* (like pitta bread) and *farinata* (pizza bread made of chickpea flour).

Vegetarians

Many Italian staples form the basis of excellent vegetarian dishes, so, although there are few restaurants devoted to non-meat eaters, you will always be able to find something on the menu. Pastas come with a variety of sauces and pizzas with a variety of toppings and even vegans should be satisfied, plus you can find delicious roasted or stuffed vegetables often served as a side dish that can be ordered as a main course.

Menu decoder

Carpaccio: finely sliced raw beef, veal or tuna.
Culurgiones: Sardinian ravioli – small pasta pockets with a variety of fillings.
Insalata caprese: salad of sliced mozzarella cheese and tomatoes with basil.
Mallodoreddus: thick shell-shaped pasta also known as *gnochetti sardi*.

NOT JUST FOR THE MICE

Home-produced *pecorino* is divine and the majority of this full-flavoured Italian brand is from Sardinia. Made from ewe's milk it can either be young and pale, semi-matured or aged: when it becomes hard and strongly flavoured.

Panadas: small pies filled with a variety of fillings, including eels.
Pane carasau: wafer-thin crispy bread that is also known as *carta da musica* or music paper.
Pane frattau: *pane carasau* topped with tomato sauce, egg and pecorino cheese.
Risotto: rice cooked in stock with meat, chicken or fish.

Pasta sauces

al arrabbiata: hot tomato sauce.
all'algherese: clam sauce.
alla carbonara: egg, bacon and cream sauce.
alla dorgalese: lamb sauce.
alla sarda: tomato sauce and spicy sausage.
pesto: basil, pine nuts, garlic and olive oil.

Pizza

Take a pizza with tomato and cheese base mix, then add the following:
Capricciosa: artichokes, ham, sausage, mushrooms and olives.
Napolitana: anchovies.
Quattro formaggi: four types of cheese.
Quattro stagioni: artichokes, ham, mushrooms and olives baked with an egg.

Prices

The price-range categories below are based on the cost of a dinner per person without drinks:

★   under 25 euros
★★   25–35 euros
★★★   over 35 euros

Cágliari

4 Mori ★★

An intimate Cágliari institution where the focus is firmly on food of the highest quality.
Via G M Angioy.
Tel: 070 650269.
Open: 10.30am and 8.30pm, until last customer leaves.

Antica Hostaria ★★★

One of the best restaurants in the capital. The menu features dishes from every region of Italy.
Via Cavour 60.
Tel: 070 665870.
Open: lunch & dinner. Closed: Sun & Aug.

Convento di San Francesco ★★

Cágliari's newest restaurant is situated under the fabulous vaulted ceiling of a former convent. The setting is almost as good as the food, enjoyed at stylishly laid tables.
Corso V Emanuele II 56.
Tel: 070 654570.
Open: 8am–2am.

Crackers ★★

This restaurant with Piedmontese cuisine is a favourite for locals at lunchtime.
Corso V Emanuele II 195.
Tel: 070 653912. Open: lunch & dinner. Closed: Wed.

Flora ★★

This elegant yet homely dining room plays host to a seasonal menu, with traditional ingredients such as wild boar.
Via Sassari 45. Tel: 070 664735. Open: lunch & dinner. Closed: Sun.

THE SOUTH

Carloforte

La Cantina ★/★★

This tiny trattoria is full of character and offers hearty portions of soup, pasta and fresh tuna, with carafes of local wine.
Via A Gramsci 34.
Tel: 0781 854588. Open: daily, lunch & dinner.

Quartu Sant'Elena ★★/★★★

The romantic setting of this old mansion and its garden is a wonderful place for dinner. Seasonal ingredients and dishes with a modern twist.
Via Dante 81. Tel: 070 881373. Open: lunch & dinner. Closed: Sun.

Pula

Byrsa ★★

Situated almost at the gates to the Nora site, this is a huge café, bar and restaurant.
Località Nora. Tel: 338 4829796. Open: 9am–late.

Su Furriadroxu ★★

Great Sardinian food accompanied by traditional music from the island make this a place not to be missed.
Via XXIV Maggio 11. Tel: 070 9245651. Open: 12.30–3pm & 7pm–late.

THE WEST

Oristano

Bussu ★/★★

With 200 seats, a variety of dining spaces and a menu packed with Italian and traditional Sardinian dishes, this is one of the friendliest and busiest options in town.
Piazza Roma 54. Tel: 078 373761. Open: Wed–Mon 7.30am–2am.

Cocco & Dessì ★★★

Probably the best restaurant in the city, with excellent seafood cuisine and desserts. *Via Tirso 31. Tel: 0783 300720. Open: lunch & dinner. Closed: Mon.*

Torregrande

Spinnaker ★/★★

The restaurant in this campsite/resort offers delicious pizzas and tasty budget dishes. *Strada Torregrande Pontile. Tel: 0783 22074. Open: May–Sept, lunch & dinner; rest of the year, dinner only.*

THE NORTHWEST

Alghero

Al Tuguri ★★

This cosy, country-style dining room offers excellent pasta, meat and fish dishes plus Catalan cream pudding, brought by the Aragonese when they founded the town. *Via Maiorca 113. Tel: 079 976772. Open: lunch & dinner. Closed: Sun.*

Angedras ★★

Seafood and traditional Sardinian dishes as well as superb sea views at Alghero's newest eatery.

Via Cavour 31. Tel: 079 9735078; www. angedrasrestaurant.it. Open: 12.30–2pm & 7.30–11pm.

Bosa

Osteria Sa Nassa ★★

You'll find this lively place serving Bosa seafood specialities at the town end of the Ponte Vecchia. *Via Lungo Temo 13. Tel: 0785 374788. Open: 12.30–3.30pm & 5–10pm.*

Castelsardo

Bounty ★★

Large family-run restaurant just beneath the castle and the best place for an evening meal in the old part of town. *Via La Marmora 12. Tel: 079 479043. Open: noon–3pm & 7pm–midnight.*

Sassari

Da Gesuino ★/★★

This restaurant has a fine reputation for local cuisine and is reasonably priced. The wines are all Sardinian. *Via Torres 17/g. Tel: 079 273392. Open: lunch & dinner. Closed: Sun.*

THE NORTHEAST

Arzachena

Lu Stazzu ★★★

With a lovely shaded terrace and Sardinian specialities, including suckling pig, wild boar and pasta with *ragu*. *Loc Picucceddu, La Cascioni. Tel: 0789 82711. Open: May–Sept, lunch & dinner.*

La Maddalena

La Grotta ★★/★★★

A huge range of fresh fish and seafood dishes near the harbour. *Via Principe di Napoli 3. Tel: 0789 737228. Open: noon–4pm & 7pm–midnight.*

Sottovento ★/★★

Family-owned, offering seafood and pasta. *Via E Dandolo 9. Tel: 0789 730037. Open: lunch & dinner. Closed: Tue.*

Porto Cervo

La Petronilla ★★/★★★

Authentic traditional Sardinian dishes in a small dining room. *Località Sa Concua 42. Tel: 0789 9213; www.lapetronilla.com. Open: evenings.*

Food and drink

Sardinian wine

They have had a long time to get the recipe for Sardinian wine right. Archaeologists have proved that they were producing this nectar during Nuraghic times and the tradition remains unbroken still. The complicated soil structure and microclimates around the island have resulted in numerous domains and vineyards that offer a full range of wines, from heavy reds to crisp whites to Champagne-style 'bubbly'.

Sardinia's most famous wine on the international scene is Canonnau, a big, robust red that makes the perfect accompaniment to the red meats and game beloved by the locals. The best are produced around Alghero, though its vines are also grown in the villages of Oliena and Ogliastra, and further south at Sarrabus-Muravera.

The island's other great name is Vermentino, a soft fruity white wine that complements the abundant fresh fish on the menu. It is a speciality of the Gallura region in the northeast of the island, inland from the Costa Smeralda.

With so many varieties of wine available it is no problem stocking your bar

A vineyard signboard

Aperitif and digestif

Italy's famous distillate is grappa, produced from grape skins in a quality ranging from ultra smooth and dry to fiery strong. Sardinia produces its own version, Filu e Ferru, that tends to err on the unsophisticated side.

For something a little more cultured, Oristano region is famous throughout Italy for Vernaccia di Oristano, a fortified wine (around 20%) that is rather like a medium dry white port or sherry and makes an excellent aperitif, or as an after-dinner drink with pastries and biscuits if grappa or Filu e Ferru is a little too strong for you.

In addition to this leading duo are a cast list of lesser, though no less enjoyable, labels that grace restaurant wine lists and supermarket shelves. In addition to Vermentino, Gallura also produces Moscato di Temio, a sweet sparkling wine, and Nebbiolo di Luras, a lighter red table wine. Conversely, to the west in Alghero, you will be able to sample Torbato, a white offering created from vines brought from Spain by the Aragonese.

Further south, the hills of Planargia in Nuoro province are known for Malvasia di Bosa, a sweet white wine, and Oristano is the home of Semidano and Neiddera. The latter is a drinkable red, and a good all-round option.

In the far south you will find the palatable red Monica di Cágliari, produced around Campidano, and Nuragus, which, as the name suggests, is the oldest variety on the island.

Where to buy

The label of Sella e Mosca dominates the market and you can visit their *enoteca* (wine shop) between Alghero and Porto Torres to buy a full range of their wines. In addition to this, there is a whole range of small vineyards scattered around the island, where you can try to buy while on your travels.

ANY OLD IRON!

The strong fiery distillate Filu e Ferru gets its strange name because it was originally produced without the knowledge of the authorities, who taxed alcohol heavily. In order to hide their bootleg liquor, farmers and others used to bury it in the ground and place a sliver of iron, or *filu e ferru*, on the surface to mark the spot.

Café society

Coffee is the lubricant that oils the wheels of Italian daily life. It punctuates the working day, starts the evening and concludes a meal.

A caffè (café) is the perfect place to sit and watch Italian life happening around you. Businessmen call in for a shot of caffeine between meetings, standing at the bar with a perfunctory nod to their peers at either side or talking avidly into mobile phones. In the late afternoon courting couples sit at tables engrossed in intimate conversation: reinforcing their mutual bonds. Then as night falls groups of friends crowd around tables to put the world to rights with a sea of waving arms and loud exclamations that sound more like argument than discussion to a non-Italian speaker.

Italian coffee does not generally lend itself to being lingered over. It needs to be drunk hot and is finished within a couple of mouthfuls, but once at a table you are never pressured to leave, so one coffee allows you front seat for as long as you enjoy the show.

Ordering etiquette

In most cafés, if you stand inside at the bar, you will need to order and pay for your drink at a till. You will then receive a ticket, which you take to the bar where the barman will serve your drink.

If you intend to sit either inside or on the outside terrace, do not go inside to order and bring the drinks out yourself as this is a big no-no! All seats are waiter serviced and this costs you a little more.

What to order

Simply order a 'caffè' and you will get the standard espresso (meaning 'pressed out'). This is a freshly brewed short, strong and black drink. But if this is too strong for you then you

Relaxing at a harbour café in Alghero

There's a huge choice of pavement cafés

have other options. Just remember that the espresso is the coffee that forms the basis of all the other Italian coffee styles.

If you want anything different you will have to master the following words:

Americano: espresso with hot water and milk

Cappuccino: espresso with frothy milk

Corretto: espresso with a dash of alcohol (perhaps grappa or brandy)

Doppia: a double espresso

Latte: espresso with hot milk

Lungo: espresso with added hot water

Machiato: espresso with a drop of milk

Ristretto: a short, extra strong espresso

Where to imbibe

Every café serves excellent coffee, but for something a little special, try:

Antico Caffè
A Cágliari institution. Period interior.
Piazza Costituzione, Cágliari.
Tel: 070 658206.

Caffè Barcellona
It has been open since just after World War II.
Via Barcellona 84, Cágliari.
Tel: 070 659712.

Caffè Latino
Set on the city walls. Great port views.
Bastioni Magellano, Alghero.
Tel: 079 976541.

Caffè Svizzero
Open since the turn of the 20th century.
Largo Carlo Felice 6, Cágliari.
Tel: 070 653784.

La Regata
Fantastic views of the harbour and the comings and goings of the yachting set.
The Port, Porto Cervo.
Tel: 0789 91312.

Sotto La Torre
Fantastic period interior.
Piazza San Giuseppe, Cágliari.
Tel: 070 653755.

Hotels and accommodation

Sardinia has a large amount of accommodation, with the bulk of the provision being in larger resort-style complexes along the coast. From May to September there are hundreds of options. However, there is a mass shutdown in mid-September, and again at the end of October until early May, leaving off-season visitors with far less choice of where to stay, though the recommendations below offer several year-round properties.

It really cannot be stressed enough that you should not travel to Sardinia between late July and the end of August without a firm booking for accommodation. It seems the whole of Italy decamps west across the Mediterranean to lounge on the beaches, and they fill up everything that is available. From May to mid-July and in September you will be able to be a little more relaxed and find accommodation as you go along if you want to.

Prices

The pricing structure in Sardinian hotels is complicated. Rooms are more expensive with a sea view, and large resort complexes or hotels converted from old mansions may have different-sized rooms with different price structures. Price rates are also divided into at least three different seasons, with prices highest in high season, matching the late June to end of August influx. Prices drop by around 30 per

cent in early June or September, and more earlier or later.

Many hotels have a minimum stay requirement, ranging from three days to a week, especially in high season, and some require that you stay half board.

Agriturismo

Agriturismo, or agrotourism, the diversification of agricultural business to combine its activities with various forms of tourist activity, started in Italy and has spread rapidly across rural Europe. In its simplest form, it is B&B at a farm or vineyard, but in many places on Sardinia there are gastronomic restaurants on site, serving excellent Sardinian cuisine, often with produce direct from the farm.

Bed and breakfast

Finding bed and breakfast accommodation on Sardinia is easy because they also use the English phrase Bed and Breakfast on their signs.

Prices

All prices here relate to the peak season and are based on the cost of a double room.

★	under 100 euros
★★	100–150 euros
★★★	150–200 euros
★★★★	over 200 euros

Cágliari

Hotel Calamosca ★★★

Cágliari's only waterfront hotel occupies a tiny bay with a small beach on the peninsula just south of town and close to Poetta beaches. There is a bus connection to the city centre or around a 20-minute walk. Restaurant on site.
Via Calamosca 50.
Tel: 070 371628;
www.hotelcalamosca.it.
Open: all year.

T Hotel ★★★

Cágliari's ultra-modern show hotel is a huge high-tech glass and steel design by Marci Piva. With a heated pool, wellness centre, bistro, restaurant and bar, plus congress centre and banqueting hall, it is an impressive city option and about 1km (²⁄₃ mile) from the old town.
Via dei Giudicati.
Tel: 070 47400;
www.thotel.it.
Open: all year.

A room at Forte Village in Pula

THE SOUTH
Pula
Forte Village ★★★★

The largest resort on Sardinia, covering 22 hectares (55 acres), and comprising seven different complexes, this award-winning Forte/Meridien property offers exceptional luxury in a couple of family bungalows or rooms. The Italianate gardens and piazzas are beautifully done and there are several restaurants and a whole range of sports and entertainment.

Santa Maria di Pula, on a peninsula south of Pula.
Tel: 070 921516;
www.fortevillage.com.
Open: Easter, then May–Sept.

Sant'Antioco
Eden Hotel ★

This small hotel sits on the main square of the town, surrounded by the bustling atmosphere, and is a 10-minute walk from the waterfront. It is an all-year option, which is great for low season visits. Though rooms are simply furnished, they have TV, fridge and A/C, there is a good simple restaurant on site.

Piazza Parrocchia 15/7.
Tel: 0781 840768;
www.albergoleden.com.
Open: all year.

THE WEST
Cabras
Sa Pedrera ★★

A small but nicely designed single-storey complex set around a garden courtyard and surrounded with verdant gardens. The rooms are simple country-style, modern, and there is an excellent restaurant. This makes a good option for Tharros, Oristano and the salt marshes.

San Giovanni di Sinis km 7.5. Tel: 0783 370040;
www.sapedrera.it.
Open: all year.

Hotel Villa Las Tronas in Alghero overlooking the bay is a grand place in which to stay

Oristano
Eleonora Bed and Breakfast di Paula Pirini ★

Set on Oristano's most important piazza, the apartment in this grand mansion has been renovated to a high standard but with respect for the building, so the archways, wooden floors and ceilings and some frescoes remain. Rooms are comfortable.
Piazza Eleonora 12.
Tel: 0783 70435;
www.eleonora-bed-and-breakfast.com.
Open: all year.

THE NORTHWEST
Alghero
Big Fish Bed and Breakfast ★

This relaxed B&B has pleasant modern furnished rooms and sits in a residential part of the modern town, about a 15-minute walk from the historic centre. A comfortable budget option.
Via Togliatti 15.
Tel: 079 977340;
www.bigfishalghero.it.
Open: all year.

Hotel Villa Las Tronas ★★★★

This 19th-century art nouveau villa set on a rocky outcrop overlooking the water is just on the southern edge of Alghero old town. It is a characterful place to stay, as it is set in its own small park, and has period furniture in the rooms plus wonderful views.
Lungamare Valencia 24.
Tel: 079 981818;
www.
hotelvillalastronas.com.
Open: all year.

THE NORTHEAST
Cannigione
Hotel del Porto ★★★

A nicely furnished small hotel overlooking the port at Cannigione. This is an excellent lower-budget option for touring the Costa Smeralda, being just on the northern edge of the resorts.
All the rooms by the waterside have good balconies.
Via Nazionale 94.
Tel: 0789 88011;
www.hoteldelporto.com.
Open: Jan–Oct.

Luogosanto
La China ★

This farm complex is a new *agriturismo* with mature olives that were first harvested in 2007. There are also pigs and a citrus grove. The lodgings are built in traditional style and are well furnished. A good country option to the east of Alghero and west of the Costa Smeralda.
Località Balaiana 136.
Tel: 335 1634627; www.
agriturismolachina.com.
Open: all year.

OFF THE BEATEN TRACK
Aritzo
Sa Muvara Hotel ★★★

A lovely little country hotel surrounded by woodland in the heart of the island. Sa Muvara has small but well-furnished rooms, gardens and a pool, plus a cosy restaurant with regional dishes featuring organic ingredients.
Fontana Rubia.
Tel: 0784 629336;
www.samuvarahotel.com.
Open: May–Sept.

Practical guide

Arriving

By air

Scheduled services: Alitalia (*www.alitalia.it*) is the national carrier for Italy and flies several services a day to Cágliari from Rome and other Italian cities. Alitalia flights to Sardinia from other countries involve a transfer in Rome or another Italian city. British Airways (*www.ba.com*) also operates direct flights from London to Cágliari.

If travelling from North America or Australasia, the simplest option would be flights into Rome for a one transfer flight on to Sardinia. Consult a travel agent or website such as *www.lastminute.com, www.ebookers.com* or *www.expedia.com* for details of routes and fares.

Low cost airlines: There are several low-cost options: Ryanair (*www.ryanair.com*) runs daily services from London Stansted, Liverpool, East Midlands and Dublin to Alghero and services from Pisa and Rome to the same town. Rival easyJet (*www.easyjet.com*) offers services from Luton airport to Cágliari and London Gatwick airport to Olbia.

Charter services: There are charter flights to Sardinia throughout the summer, with services running from April to October for terms of one or two weeks. Contact the major package tourist companies such as Thomas Cook (*tel: in the UK 0870 750 5711; www.thomascook.co.uk*) for more

details. These companies sell holiday packages (flight and accommodation) but also sell flight-only tickets to travellers who want to arrange their accommodation themselves.

By sea

Travelling with your own car from mainland Europe makes a lot of sense. There are numerous crossings from the Italian peninsula, the closest being a departure from Genoa. Grand Navi Veloci (*www.gnv.it*) runs a daily overnight service from this port to Porto Torres in the north of Sardinia, with comfortable cabins, restaurants and bars.

There are also services from France with SNCM (*www.sncm.fr*) via Corsica. This is the shortest driving/ferry route to the island.

For details and times of ferry services see the *Thomas Cook European Rail Timetable*, published monthly, available to buy online at *www.thomascookpublishing.com* or from branches of Thomas Cook in the UK (*tel: 01733 416477*).

Entry formalities

EU citizens need only a picture ID to gain entry. Residents of the following countries need a valid passport: UK, Australia, Canada, New Zealand and the USA. All other nationalities should consult the nearest Italian Embassy about entry requirements.

Camping

There are excellent camping facilities on Sardinia with sites all around the coastline; many are close to the best beaches and the towns for easy sightseeing. Some sites have dated facilities and they can get very crowded in high season. Campsites will charge for all extras, including hot showers. On some sites cars must be parked in a separate area after you have pitched your tent or parked your caravan.

Campsites usually have chalets that can be rented by the day or the week with bedding and cooking facilities. This can be an excellent option for travellers on a budget.

Most campsites close by the end of September, reopening in April, though more and more are staying open all year.

Tourist offices have details of all campsites in their area.

Climate

Sardinia has a Mediterranean maritime climate with hot, dry summers and mild winters. The bulk of rainfall takes place between October and December and tends to fall in passing storms.

Crime

When you visit Sardinia you will be at a relatively low risk of being a victim of serious crime. However, so-called petty crime such as theft can be a problem, especially from vehicles. It still pays to take precautions to minimise your chances of a loss:

- Do not leave valuables in a car and leave nothing at all on show.
- Do not carry large amounts of cash or valuables with you.
- Deposit valuables in the hotel safe.
- Take extra care at cashpoint machines; do not allow bystanders to see your PIN.
- Put all money away before you leave banks or bureau de change kiosks.
- Carry handbags across your body.
- Do not leave valuables unattended in cafés and restaurants.

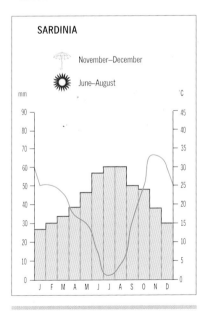

SARDINIA

November–December

June–August

WEATHER CONVERSION CHART

25.4mm = 1 inch

°F = 1.8 × °C + 32

Customs regulations

The following duty-free rules apply for visitors arriving from outside the EU: 400 cigarettes or 500g (17^1/2 oz) tobacco, 1 litre of spirits or 2 litres of table wine.

Travellers from other EU countries can import unlimited amounts of alcohol, tobacco and perfume for their personal use. There are no currency restrictions.

Driving

Bringing your own vehicle into Sardinia

Carry the registration document, valid insurance and valid licence. It is compulsory to carry two warning triangles in case of accident, which need to be placed some distance in front and behind the car to warn

The signposting can be a little confusing

other traffic. Wear a reflective waistcoat (compulsory) if you break down in bad visibility or at night. Headlights should be switched on at all times, even during the day.

Car rental

A full national or an international driving licence will be needed for rental. The minimum age for rental is 21 with a full licence for at least one year (25 for some companies or types of vehicle).

Carry your driver's licence and rental document at all times.

Fuel

Self-service fuel stations can be found at all towns and on the two-lane highways. Note that most close for lunch and siesta between around 1pm to around 4pm, but they have automatic machines that take credit cards or euro notes. Petrol stations normally stay open until around 9pm.

General rules

Drive on the right and pass on the left. Most main roads have good surfaces. Minor roads may be uneven and narrow with limited vision, blind bends and hidden entrances. Road signs and markings comply with the European standard. Alcohol limits are 0.5mg per 100ml of blood. Children under 12 should be seated in the back. Seat belts must be worn by all passengers.

Parking
This is difficult in most large towns.

Speed limits
Urban/villages 50kph (31mph).
All other roads 90kph (56mph).
Two-lane highways 110kph (68mph).
Lower in wet weather.
Specific limits may apply especially in
towns, so keep an eye on speed signs.

Electricity
220 volt with European-style two-pin
plugs. If you are travelling from the UK
you will need an adaptor plug.

Embassies/consulates
All embassies are located in Rome on
the Italian mainland.
Australia Via Antonio Bosio 5, I-00161
Roma. *Tel: 06 85272 1;*
fax: 06 85272 300;
www.italy.embassy.gov.au
Canada Via Zara 30, I-00198 Roma.
Tel: 06 85 4441; fax: 06 85 444 2905.
New Zealand Via Zara 28, I-00186
Roma. *Tel: 06 441 7171;*
fax: 06 440 2984; www.nzembassy.com
Republic of Ireland Piazza di
Campitelli 3, I-00186 Roma.
Tel: 06 697 9121; fax: 06 697 2354;
www.foreignaffairs.gov.ie
South Africa Via Tanaro 14, I-0019
Roma. *Tel: 06 85 2541;*
fax: 06 8525 4258; www.sudafrica.it
UK
Via XX Settembre 80a, I-00187 Roma.
Tel: 06 4220 0001; fax: 06 4220 2347;
www.britishembassy.gov.uk

CONVERSION TABLE

FROM	TO	MULTIPLY BY
Inches	Centimetres	2.54
Feet	Metres	0.3048
Yards	Metres	0.9144
Miles	Kilometres	1.6090
Acres	Hectares	0.4047
Gallons	Litres	4.5460
Ounces	Grams	28.35
Pounds	Grams	453.6
Pounds	Kilograms	0.4536
Tons	Tonnes	1.0160

To convert back, for example from
centimetres to inches, divide by the number
in the third column.

MEN'S SUITS

UK	36	38	40	42	44	46	48
Rest of Europe	46	48	50	52	54	56	58
USA	36	38	40	42	44	46	48

DRESS SIZES

UK	8	10	12	14	16	18
France	36	38	40	42	44	46
Italy	38	40	42	44	46	48
Rest of Europe	34	36	38	40	42	44
USA	6	8	10	12	14	16

MEN'S SHIRTS

UK	14	14.5	15	15.5	16	16.5	17
Rest of Europe	36	37	38	39/40	41	42	43
USA	14	14.5	15	15.5	16	16.5	17

MEN'S SHOES

UK	7	7.5	8.5	9.5	10.5	11
Rest of Europe	41	42	43	44	45	46
USA	8	8.5	9.5	10.5	11.5	12

WOMEN'S SHOES

UK	4.5	5	5.5	6	6.5	7
Rest of Europe	38	38	39	39	40	41
USA	6	6.5	7	7.5	8	8.5

British Honorary Consulate, Viale Colombo 160, I-09045 Quartu S Elena, Cágliari. *Tel/fax: 070 813412.*

USA

Via Vittorio Veneto 119/A, I-00187 Roma. *Tel: 06 4674 1;*
fax: 06 4674 2356;
www.italy.usembassy.gov

Emergency telephone numbers

The emergency numbers are:
National Police (Polizia Nationale): *113*
Police (Carabinieri): *112*
Fire brigade (Vigili del Fuoco): *115*
Ambulance (Ambulanza): *118*

Health

There are no compulsory inoculations for travel to Sardinia.

Medical provision is of a high standard, with most staff speaking some English. The water is potable, but bottled water tastes better.

Pharmacies (*farmacia*) sell many drugs over the counter. However, brand names vary, so if you need a specific medication/drug take an empty packet with you to aid the pharmacist or carry a prescription from your doctor.

Insurance

Having adequate health insurance cover is vital. UK citizens with a European Health Insurance Card (available online at *www.ehic.org.uk,* from the post office or *tel: 0845 606 2030*) will be treated without charge, but a travel insurance policy will allow repatriation if the injuries or illness warrant it. All other nationalities should ensure adequate cover for illness, as they will be charged at point of treatment.

Travellers should always have cover for everything they carry with them in case of loss or theft.

Insurance companies also usually provide cover for cancellation or travel delay in their policies. Though not essential, this cover offers some compensation if travel plans go awry.

Language

The national language of Sardinia is Italian, but many inhabitants also speak the native language, Sardinian, and a few around Alghero still speak Catalan, another Romance language that was brought with the Aragonese from northern Spain. Sardinian is spoken more in the country than in the cities and towns and everyone speaks Italian. See page 185 for a few hints in Italian to get you started.

Lost property

You will need an official police report to make an insurance claim for any lost property. If you lose your passport, you will have to contact your embassy or consulate immediately.

Maps

The tourist offices in the major towns have maps of their respective areas, though finding the tourist office so that you can obtain a map can prove problematical! Basic touring maps

Language

Pronunciation

All letters are pronounced as in English unless indicated below.

Letters	Pronunciation in Italian
c	*Pronounced hard before a, o and u but 'ch' before e and i*
ch	*Pronounced 'k'*
g	*Pronounced hard as in 'go' before a, o and u, soft as in 'jet' before e and i*
gh	*Pronounced as hard g*
gli	*Pronounced 'lyi' as the 'lli' in stallion*
gn	*Pronounced 'ny', so signora is pronounced seen-yoh'rah*
h	*Always silent*
r	*Always rolled*
sc	*Pronounced 'sk' before h, a, o and u, 'sh' before e and i*
sch	*Pronounced 'sk'*
z	*Pronounced 'ts' except when it starts a word, then 'ds'*

Stress and inflection

Stress is a very important element in being able to speak Italian like a local. Stress falls on the second to last syllable of a word unless the word contains an accent, in which case stress falls on the syllable with the accent. Where words contain a double consonant this elongates that sound within the word and places stress on the sound of the double letter

HELPFUL PHRASES

English	Italian	English	Italian
Hello	Buon giorno or Ciao (familiar)	Large/Big	Grande
Goodbye	Arrivederci or Ciao (familiar)	Small	Piccolo
Yes	Si	Good	Buono
No	No	Bad	Cattivo
Do you speak English?	Parla inglese?	Well	Bene
I don't understand	Non capisco	Everything's fine	Va' bene
Where is the?	Dove es …?	Too much	Troppo
How much is it?	Quanto costa?	Very much	Molto
Please	Per favore	Enough	Basta
Thank you	Grazie	Open	Aperto
One	Uno	Closed	Chiuso
Two	Due	Ticket	Biglietto
Three	Tre	Entrance	Entrata
Four	Quattro	Exit	Uscita
Five	Cinque	Left	Sinistra
Six	Sei	Right	Destra
Seven	Sette	Please (don't mention it), which is the invariable response to 'grazie' or thanks	Prego
Eight	Otto		
Nine	Nove	Excuse me! (eg when moving through a crowd)	Permesso!
Ten	Dieci		
One hundred	Cento	Excuse me (apology)	Mi scusi

can be picked up from the car rental companies, but for a detailed map try a good bookshop.

Media

Sardinia has two daily newspapers, *L'Unione Sarda,* which includes a short English-language section, and *La Nuova Sardegna.* The British tabloids and broadsheets are available from *tabacchi* in Cágliari and Alghero, and occasionally at other resorts around the island.

Money matters

ATMs

ATMs are becoming more numerous and you will certainly be able to get cash in the major towns. Make sure you have a Personal Identification Number (PIN) that is recognised by machines abroad. If unsure contact your bank.

Credit cards

Credit cards are widely accepted across Sardinia. The most popular are MasterCard and VISA. You can also use your credit card to get cash advances over the counter in banks.

Currency

The currency of Italy (Sardinia) is the euro. One euro is made up of one hundred cents. Coins come in denominations of 1, 2, 5, 10, 20 and

News-stands stock a wide range of reading material

50 cents, 1 and 2 euros. Notes are in denominations of 5, 10, 20, 50, 100, 200 and 500 euros.

Currency exchange

All banks and post offices on Sardinia will exchange currency (*cambio*) and commission rates are generally low. Commercial bureau de change will also exchange but will charge a higher commission fee than a bank.

Traveller's cheques

These are the safest way to carry holiday cash as they can be replaced if they are lost or stolen. You can change these at hotels, or at bureaux de change and banks, but the same advice applies about commission rates as with cash above.

Opening hours

Shops generally 9am–1pm and 4–8pm Monday–Saturday. Shops in tourist resorts stay open throughout the day in the tourist season and may close completely in winter.

Large supermarkets daily 9am–8pm.
Small supermarkets have the same opening hours except Sunday 9am–1pm.

Post offices Monday–Friday 8.15am–5pm and Saturday 8.30am–noon or 1pm. Post offices close early on the last day of the month.

Banks Monday–Friday 9am–1pm.
Museums Varying opening hours but mainly daily 9am–8pm mid-July–early

September, Tuesday–Saturday 9am–1pm, 4–8pm rest of the year.
Pharmacies 9am–12.30pm and 3.30–7.30pm. There are duty pharmacies in the major towns.

Police

Policing is a complicated business in Italy and there is a lot of duplication of roles and responsibilities. There is the Polizia Nationale (uniform of navy tunic with light blue trousers), a civil force overseen by the Interior Ministry, and the Carabinieri (black uniform with red piping), who report to the Ministry of Defence. Both forces deal with public order and street crime. For parking offences you will deal with the Vigili Urbani or local traffic police.

In an emergency contact the Polizia Nationale (*tel: 113*) or Carabinieri (*tel: 112*).

Post offices

Post offices (*La Posta*) can be found in all major towns. Service is not speedy but it is improving. Opening times are generally Monday to Friday 8.15am–5pm and Saturday 8.30am–noon or 1pm. Post offices close early on the last day of the month.

Local tobacconists (*tabacchi*) also sell stamps (*francobolli*) and this might be easier than trying to find a post office.

Public holidays

The following dates are official holidays in Italy, but some dates are movable – so check with the tourist office. All government buildings, banks and most commercial businesses will be closed.

1 January New Year's Day
6 January Epiphany
March/April Easter Monday
25 April Liberation Day
1 May Labour Day
15 August Assumption Day
1 November All Saints' Day
8 December Immaculate Conception
25 December Christmas Day
26 December St Stephen's Day

Public transport

The island has a rail network that links the major towns. For details of services consult Italian national railways' website *www.trenitalia.it* (in Italian). These services are not practical for reaching the countryside, but bus services do link smaller towns and villages from the main urban centres. Azienda Regionale Sarda Transporti, or ARST, runs services to the larger towns with several smaller regional companies linking with ARST services.
Via Zagabria 54, Cágliari.
Tel: 800 865042.

Details of local rail services are shown in the *Thomas Cook European Rail Timetable*, published monthly, available to buy online at *www.thomascookpublishing.com* or from branches of Thomas Cook in the UK (*tel: 01733 416477*).

Sustainable tourism

Thomas Cook is a strong advocate of ethical and fairly traded tourism and believes that the travel experience should be as good for the places visited as it is for the people that visit. That's why we're a firm supporter of The Travel Foundation: a charity that develops solutions to help improve and protect holiday destinations, their environment, traditions and culture. To find out what you can do to make a positive difference to the places you travel to and the people who live there, please visit *www.thetravelfoundation.org.uk*

Telephones

Modern hotels will usually have a direct-dial phone system, but they often charge extortionate surcharges for calls. Ask about charges before you make the decision to ring home.

The country code for Italy is 039, and all Sardinian numbers have nine or ten digits. Here are the main country codes should you want to make an international call from Sardinia.
Australia 00 61
Ireland 00 353
New Zealand 00 64
UK 00 44
USA and Canada 00 1

Public phones are now almost 100 per cent card (credit card or phonecard) operated. You can buy phonecards from news kiosks and tobacconists (*tabacchi*).

Mobile (cell) phone coverage is good in the main towns and along main highways. Check with your mobile phone company for details (cost and partner provision) of their service on Sardinia.

Time

Sardinia works to Central European time, which is one hour ahead of Greenwich Mean Time in winter and two hours ahead in summer. If it is one o'clock in Cágliari it is noon in London.

Tipping

Tipping is not expected in restaurants where service is already added to the bill. Where it is not, a 10–15 per cent tip should be given. In bars and cafés it is customary to leave small change. Always tip porters and room cleaners.

Toilets

Toilets are generally of a good clean standard but there are few public facilities. The best policy is to use the facilities of a café or bar.

Tourist information

Tourist information across the island is patchy. The major towns have offices that are open all year, while resorts have seasonal offices or kiosks usually open July–August. Sardinian communes run Pro Loco information offices, which will usually have maps and information on where to stay, but most have very little information in English. For information before you arrive consult the Italian Tourist Board website *www.enit.it* or the following Sardinia-specific commercial websites:

www.sarnow.com/sardinia or *www.sardinia.net*

Travellers with disabilities

Provision for travellers with mobility problems is variable. New buildings have to meet a code standard for wheelchair access and some others have been adapted. Always make specific enquiries with hotels if you require specially equipped rooms. By the very nature of their natural attractions, some areas will be difficult to access.

For more holiday and travel information for people with disabilities contact: *Holiday Care Services, tel: 0845 124 9971 (UK); www.holidaycare.org.uk*

The Tourist Information Centre in Cágliari

Index

Acknowledgements

Thomas Cook wishes to thank the photographers, picture libraries and other organisations for the loan of the photographs reproduced in this book, to whom copyright in the photographs belongs.

PETE BENNETT 5a & b, 8, 10, 16, 17, 18, 20, 21, 22, 23, 24, 25, 26, 27, 31, 34, 35, 38, 39, 41, 42, 43, 45, 49, 50, 51, 56, 57, 61, 62, 63, 64, 65, 67, 72, 73, 76, 77, 78, 80, 81, 82, 95, 101, 102, 103, 105, 114, 115, 118, 119, 132, 137, 138, 140, 141, 142, 143, 147, 148, 151, 156, 161, 163, 165, 166, 167, 172, 173, 178
MARC DI DUCA 15, 19, 33, 40, 47, 48, 58, 69, 96, 97, 99, 107, 116, 121, 149, 153, 155, 159, 164, 182, 186, 189
FLICKR/cristianocani 44, piglicker 66, 177, the summer is magic 84, 89, Corydora 91, Gaspart 124, Roby Ferrari 131, clurr 145
FOTOLIA/David Harding 94
THOMAS COOK PUBLISHING 9, 11, 32, 157, 175
WIKIMEDIA COMMONS/Fawcett5 87
WORLD PICTURES/PHOTOSHOT 1, 86, 100, 106, 122, 123, 125, 127, 135, 160, 174

For CAMBRIDGE PUBLISHING MANAGEMENT LTD:
Project editor: Rosalind Munro
Proofreader: Ian Faulkner
Typesetter: Julie Crane

SEND YOUR THOUGHTS TO
BOOKS@THOMASCOOK.COM

We're committed to providing the very best up-to-date information in our travel guides and constantly strive to make them as useful as they can be. You can help us to improve future editions by letting us have your feedback. If you've made a wonderful discovery on your travels that we don't already feature, if you'd like to inform us about recent changes to anything that we do include, or if you simply want to let us know your thoughts about this guidebook and how we can make it even better – we'd love to hear from you.

Send us ideas, discoveries and recommendations today and then look out for your valuable input in the next edition of this title.

Emails to the above address, or letters to Travellers Series Editor, Thomas Cook Publishing, PO Box 227, Coningsby Road, Peterborough PE3 8SB, UK.

Please don't forget to let us know which title your feedback refers to!